The NCO-ER Leadership Guide

By Wilson L. Walker

Becoming a Better Leader and Getting Promoted in Today's Army

The Complete Guide to the New NCO-ER

The NCO-ER Leadership Guide

The Self-Development Test Study Guide

Up or Out: How to Get Promoted as the Army Draws Down

The NCO-ER
Leadership Guide

Wilson L. Walker
Master Sergeant, U.S. Army, Retired

IMPACT PUBLICATIONS
Manassas Park, Virginia

ISBN: 1-57023-224-5

Library of Congress: 2004104216

Publisher: For information on Impact Publications, including current and forthcoming publications, authors, press kits, online bookstore, and submission requirements, visit the left navigation bar on the front page of our main company website: www.impactpublications.com.

Publicity/Rights: For information on publicity, author interviews, and subsidiary rights, contact the Media Relations Department: Tel. 703-361-7300, Fax 703-335-9486, or email: info@impactpublications.com.

Sales/Distribution: All special sales and distribution inquiries should be directed to the publisher: Sales Department, IMPACT PUBLICATIONS, 9104 Manassas Drive, Suite N, Manassas Park, VA 20111-5211, Tel. 703-361-7300, Fax 703-335-9486, or email: info@impactpublications.com.

Contents

Preface

N O MATTER HOW YOU LOOK at it, the Army has a new mission. Today's soldiers have become the peacekeepers of the world. Taking on new homeland security roles, they are often stretched so thin that the federal government now pays civilians to check cars as they enter military bases so Army guards can get back to their traditional jobs as well as be ready to deploy if called upon.

Thousands upon thousands of National Guards – "citizen soldiers" – are also being called to active duty. In between the many PCS moves and other hardships, the soldier still has to attend leadership schools to be promoted, if he or she plans to remain on active duty or retire some day from a military career. While going into a combat zone will not get you promoted, assessments made by your rater and senior rater about your performance in the combat zone are what will get you promoted and into good assignments.

Don't just sit back and let the new fast-paced Army leave you behind. Be proactive and read this book and its companion volume, *The Complete Guide to the New NCO-ER*, to learn what you should know about the new NCO-ER and how to receive or write a good report.

If you want to have a successful military career, be sure to take control of your NCO-ER today!

1

You As an Army Leader

T HERE ARE TWO CLASSIFICATIONS of leaders in the Army: the commissioned officer and the non-commissioned officer. The commissioned officers (Lt-Gen) are appointed by the President of the United States to act as his legal agent and help carry out his duties as the Commander-in-Chief. They get their legal authority from the president. The non-commissioned officers' authority is delegated to them by the commissioned officer, which means the NCOs serve as agents for the commissioned officers.

Authority is the legitimate power of leaders to direct soldiers or to take action within the scope of their responsibility. NCOs also have command and general military authority. The Army's mission demands that officers and NCOs work together. When they work together they learn from each other. The commissioned officers must give the NCOs the guidance, resources, assistance, and supervision necessary for them to do their duties.

The NCOs are responsible for assisting and advising officers in carrying out their duties. They also advise commanders on individual soldiers' proficiency and training needed to ensure unit readiness. This leaves the commander free to plan, make decisions, and program future training and operations. The officers plan and decide what needs to be done, and the NCOs make sure it gets done. The major role of the NCO is the care of the soldiers and training. How they care for the soldiers has changed somewhat due to the huge advances in technology and quality-of-life programs.

There is, however, another type of army leader — the warrant officer. They are appointed by the Secretary of the Army and get their authority from the same person as the officers if they are placed in a command position.

> *The major role of the NCO is the care of the soldiers and training.*

The NCOs of today's Army must be well educated so they can understand, speak, and execute the directives of the officers; they must also enforce the standards and be a role model for others to follow. NCOs are now being placed in a combat role more challenging than ever before. When they find themselves the only leader present on the battlefield, they must be able to execute the intent of officers in order to achieve success. They must be bold, take risks, and be selfless and totally professional. They must also be able to take the initiative in the absence of a commissioned officer, and execute and accomplish the mission.

The Army doctrine demands that the NCO be proficient in all leadership competencies and Army values. As a leader (NCO) the Army expects you to:

- Influence your soldiers to accomplish the unit's mission.
- Give your soldiers a reason for what you want them to do.
- Provide direction by telling them how you want something done.
- Motivate your soldiers to want to accomplish the mission.
- Teach your soldiers the Army values.

- Strive to master your job and prepare to take your leadership position.
- Do what is right to achieve excellence.
- Bear true faith and allegiance to the U.S. Constitution, Army, unit, and soldiers.
- Fulfill your obligations, morally and professionally right.
- Treat people with respect, as they should be treated.
- Put the welfare of the nation, Army, and soldiers before your own.
- Live up to all the Army values.
- Do what is right, legally and morally.
- Become an aggressive thinker, always anticipating and analyzing.
- Face fear, danger, or adversity.
- Become a self-disciplined NCO.
- Make sound and good judgments.
- Have self-confidence.
- Have the intellectual ability to think, learn, and reflect.
- Be sensitive to the different backgrounds of your soldiers.
- Be aware of the culture of the overseas country in which you are stationed.
- Take account of the customs and traditions wherever you are stationed.
- Maintain the appropriate level of physical fitness and military bearing.
- Maintain calm under pressure, and expend energy on things you can fix.
- Invest your energy in self-improvement.
- Stay abreast of advances that enhance tactical abilities.
- Take care of your soldiers by maximizing their performance.
- Adjust your leadership style to the situation.
- Focus on personnel and family concerns.
- Control your fears, anger, despair, and panic.
- Listen to and care for the soldiers.
- Know and deal with soldiers' perception.
- Set examples for your soldiers to follow.
- Keep your soldiers productively busy.

- Reward positive contributions with a pat on the back.
- Act decisively in the face of panic.
- Learn about leaders and other soldiers.
- Be able to cope with the fear of unknown injury and death.
- Share ideas and feelings freely with leaders and soldiers.
- Maintain and sustain trust and confidence.
- Assist soldiers to deal with immediate problems.
- Respond to soldiers' problems.
- Establish individual and unit goals.
- Build pride and spirit through the unit activities.
- Build pride through accomplishments.
- Learn all you can about the battlefield.
- Overcome family-versus-unit conflicts.
- Acquire habits of self-evaluation/self-assessment.
- Know yourself and your soldiers.
- Set reachable goals for your soldiers.
- Remain flexible when trying to make sense of your experiences.
- Help your organization excel to become the best.
- Explain and/or show your soldiers how to succeed.
- Have the ability to sort through vast amounts of information.
- Assess tactical training and set the example.
- Becomes a master at influencing your soldiers.
- Know your boss's intent, priorities, and thought process.
- Choose and execute the best solution to problems.
- Determine objectives that are specific and measurable.
- Prioritize the tasks to be accomplished.
- Have the ability to assess a situation accurately and reliably.
- Obtain information from various sources to compare and make a sound judgment.
- Compare the relative efficiency or effectiveness against Army standards.
- Teach soldiers to do the leader's job in combat.
- Take time to allow soldiers to develop ways to meet organizational missions.
- Routinely weld soldiers together for mission accomplishments.
- Deal with diversity, complexity, ambiguity, change, uncertainty, and conflicting policies.

- Look realistically at what the future may hold.
- Incorporate new ideas, new technologies, and new capabilities.
- Provide the ultimate sense of purpose, direction, and motivation.
- Operate in an environment of increased volatility, uncertainty, complexity, and ambiguity.

This list of what the Army expects you to do is only part of the many things that will be expected of you. Look over the list again and ask yourself, *"Can I accomplish that task?"* To become the leader the Army and your rating official will recognize, you must be the leader they will accept. In order for you to become that acceptable leader the Army is looking for, you first need to know yourself.

Know Yourself

To know yourself is to know your values, beliefs, and ethics. It is doing a 100% true evaluation of yourself which only you can do. After you evaluate yourself you will be able to form a relationship with your boss and soldiers that can make you the successful leader the Army and rating official want you to become, one who can train his/her soldiers for combat and to accomplish the unit's, Army's, and nation's objectives. Your boss wants a leader who can run things when he/she is away, someone who can train and care for the soldiers, and someone who has some of the same values and beliefs. The soldiers on the other hand want someone whom they can look up to, a leader whom they can respect and one who will, in turn, respect them. They want a leader who will reward them when they exceed the standards and one who will stand up for them when they need support and train them so they can accomplish the Army's mission and, if need be, return home from combat.

> *The more you know about yourself, the better your chances are of becoming the leader the Army and rating official want.*

The more you know about yourself, the better your chances are of becoming the leader the Army and rating official want. Evaluate yourself by asking the following questions:

1. Am I being counseled about my NCO-ER?
2. Have I updated my duty description?
3. Is my NCO-ER rating official correct?
4. Do I know what is necessary for a successful rating?
5. Is all my administrative data correct on DA form 2166-8?
6. Did I write down key points during my NCO-ER counseling?
7. Am I aware of developmental counseling in FM 22-100, appendix C?
8. Do I know my NCO-ER official rating chain?
9. Do I know the meaning of the Army values?
10. Do I know how the Army values apply to my daily duties?
11. Do I have examples for NCO-ER excellence rating?
12. Are my counseling dates recorded on DA form 2166-8-1?
13. Am I aware of my action and behavior during the rating period?
14. Am I aware of what has happened, been done, and can be done better?
15. Am I being recognized for special emphasis on my NCO-ER?
16. Am I a competent NCO?
17. Am I physically fit?
18. How is my military bearing?
19. Can I influence my soldiers?
20. What is my leadership style?
21. What type of leader am I?
22. Am I able to lead others?
23. Do I meet or exceed all standards?
24. When is my next NCO-ER due?
25. When is my next NCO-ER counseling due?
26. What are my daily duties and scope?
27. What are my areas of special emphasis?
28. What are my appointed duties?
29. Are my counseling dates correct on DA form 2166-8?
30. Am I loyal to the Army, unit, and soldiers?

31. Do I treat people with respect?
32. Do I put the welfare of the nation, Army, and soldiers before mine?
33. Do I live up to the Army values?
34. Do I do what is legally and morally right?
35. Do I have the courage to face fear, danger, and adversity?
36. Am I proficient and competent in my assigned duties?
37. Do I have the technical and tactical knowledge needed for my MOS?
38. Do I make sound judgments?
39. Do I seek self-improvement?
40. Do I accomplish tasks to their fullest?
41. Am I committed to excellence?
42. How is my mental and physical toughness?
43. Do I have the endurance and stamina to go the distance?
44. Do I display confidence and enthusiasm?
45. Do I put the mission first?
46. Do I have genuine concern for the soldiers?
47. Do I instill the spirit to achieve and win?
48. Do I set the example of Be, Know, and Do?
49. Am I a good individual and team trainer?
50. Do I stay focused on the mission?
51. Am I performance-oriented?
52. Do I share my knowledge and experience?
53. Do I care for and maintain the equipment and facilities?
54. Am I concerned with soldiers' and equipment safety?
55. Am I conservative with supplies and funds?
56. Do I take responsibility for good, bad, right, and wrong?
57. What is my potential for promotion?
58. Am I ready for more responsibility?
59. Am I ready for the next higher grade?
60. How am I doing on the APFT?
61. Are my height and weight IAW within the Army standards?
62. Can my boss and soldiers rely on me?
63. Do I make decisions just to please my leaders?
64. Is my education level in line with my grade level?
65. Do I over- or under-supervise my soldiers?

The list of things that the Army expects you to do, to become a good soldier, is somewhat different from the list of things that you should ask yourself when you do a self-evaluation. The list of things you should ask yourself when doing an evaluation is more important for two reasons than the list of things the Army expects you to do:

1. The evaluation list covers all that the Army expects you to do.
2. The evaluation list includes things that your rating official will rate you on.

> *No matter how good a leader you think you are, it is what your rating official says about you that counts.*

No matter how good a leader you may think you are, it is what your rating official says about you that counts. Your leadership skills must be mentioned on your NCO-ER, which would explain the type of leader you are, as seen by your rater and senior rater, which in turn will be believed by the Army or the Department of the Army. We will discuss this in more detail later. For now let's look at Army values.

Know the Army Values

Your values are the personal, private, and individual beliefs you hold about what is important to you. Values govern your entire lifestyle, from the way you dress, the car you drive, your leadership style, to the food you eat, and even how you raise your children or lead your soldiers. Your values will also influence your priorities and decisions. The seven Army values that all soldiers are expected to possess are:

1. **LOYALTY** is to bear true faith and allegiance to the U.S. Constitution, the Army, your unit, and other soldiers. Loyalty is a two-way street; so do not expect what you yourself do not give (respect). The loyalty of your soldiers is the greatest gift you can receive from them. Through their loyalty to you, they give you permission to train and lead them through combat and return them home to their loved ones.

We were on a three-day field trip in West Germany, when I had to return to the unit to pick up some TA-50 that was on a truck which had broken down and been returned to the motor pool.

By the time I got the TA-50 off the truck, I was so tired that I told the C.Q. I was going to lie down in the day room, and asked him to wake me up in a half-hour or so. After he woke me up I headed back to the field location. Since I was still sleepy, I stopped at a bowling alley to get a cup of coffee. When I walked in, I could smell hot dogs and hamburgers cooking on the grill.

The next day, I was sitting with my soldiers eating some MREs and talking. I told them about how I happened to stop at the bowling alley the previous day to get a cup of coffee and how good the hot dogs and hamburgers smelled. Then I asked them if they believed I had a hamburger with my cup of coffee. One of the soldiers looked at me and said, "Sergeant Walker, there was no way you would have a burger without bringing all of us one back." I did not think about it at the time, but that shows loyalty.

2. **DUTY** is no more than "fulfill your obligations." Duty begins with everything required of you by law.

Another time when I was stationed in Germany, I was placed in one of the units as "acting first sergeant." During my short stay there I had a weigh-in set up for the company. One of the NCOs did not want to be weighed in; he was an E-8 and I was an E-7. Knowing my position as the first sergeant overrode his grade, I gave him an order to be weighed in. He turned out to be overweight and I had him placed on the overweight program. As the acting first sergeant, it was my duty to not only set up the weigh-in but also to put anyone who did not meet the standards on the overweight program.

3. **RESPECT** is treating people as they should be treated. Respect means recognizing and appreciating the inherent dignity and worth of all people. As a leader you will deal with soldiers from a wide range of ethnic, racial, and religious backgrounds. You show your soldiers respect by seeking to understand their background, seeing

things from their perspective, and appreciating what is important to them.

> I was a section chief in West Germany at the time and had just gotten a new soldier in my section. A day or two before we had a four-day weekend coming up, my new soldier walked up to me and asked for a four-day pass so that he could go to a rock concert. He explained that he did not know anything about Germany, but he did know about the bands for the concert. As he talked to me about going to the concert, I could see how much it meant to him. I had never been to a rock concert and did not like rock bands or music, but, since he did, I let him go. I was able to set my feelings aside and view the situation from his perspective. As it turned out, during the time we were together he became one of the best soldiers in the section. As a leader, it is important that you learn to put your beliefs and feelings aside and respect those of your soldiers and others.

4. **SELFLESS-SERVICE** is putting the welfare of the nation, Army, and soldiers before your own. Selfless-service means doing what is right for the nation, Army, your organization, and your soldiers, and putting these responsibilities above your own interests. This does not mean neglecting your family or yourself; it does not mean that you cannot have a strong ego, high self-esteem, or even healthy ambition. The selfless leader gives credit to those who earned it, which brings me back to the soldier who wanted the four-day pass to attend the rock concert.

> I was the section chief of a "HAWK" missile maintenance (24D) section. One time we had a radar that was down and had been down for a day or two. I had been working on the radar all night alone with my warrant officer and a man from the Raytheon Company. My rock concert soldier came up to the radar the next morning to relieve me; about a half-hour later he came down to the section and said that he had fixed the radar. After we all went up to check it out, we discovered, that it was indeed fixed. As I was walking back down to the section I saw the commander, who told me thanks and said I had done a good job fixing the radar. I told the commander that my soldier had fixed the radar and asked him

to thank the soldier — which he did. While it is ok to look out for yourself, give credit where it is due, and it all will come back to you.

5. **HONOR** is living up to all the Army values. Honor holds Army values together while at the same time being a value itself. To be an honorable person, you must be true to your oath and live the Army values in all you do. When you are an Army leader, honor means putting Army values above self-interest, above career, and above comfort for all soldiers; it also means putting Army values above self-preservation.

One time I had a lot of accumulated leave to take, but a big field problem surfaced. Since I was the platoon sergeant I wanted to be with my platoon. I made the choice to go to the field, but when the first sergeant told the commander about it, he gave me time off for the days I lost. At the time I did not think about putting Army values above self-interest; I just wanted to be there with my platoon.

6. **INTEGRITY** is doing what is right, legally and morally. Having integrity means being both morally complete and true to one's self. As an Army leader, you are always on display. If you want to instill Army values in others, you must internalize and demonstrate them yourself. Any conflict between your personal values and Army values must be resolved before you can become a morally complete Army leader. Conducting yourself with integrity has three parts:

   1. Separating what is right from what is wrong.
   2. Always acting according to what you know to be right, even at personal cost.
   3. Saying openly that you are acting on your understanding of right versus wrong.

One thing I enjoyed doing in Germany was running up and down the hills there, and one of the best places to run was in Fulda, where they had a half and full marathon each year. One day the battalion commander came down to the unit, and before he left he called me into the commander's office and asked about my running. He told the commander to let me off from work any time I wanted to go train. If I wanted to, I could take off each day and go run, but I did not, because my soldiers, who played sports also, could not get off to train, so I just kept doing my training after duty hours and on the weekends.

7. **PERSONAL COURAGE** is facing fear, danger, or adversity. Personal courage is not the absence of fear; rather, it is the ability to put fear aside and do what is necessary. Physical courage means overcoming fear of bodily harm and doing your duty. In contrast, moral courage is the willingness to stand firm on your values, principles, and convictions even when threatened. Leaders who take responsibility for their actions and decisions, even when things go wrong, display moral courage. Moral courage often expresses itself as candor. Candor means being frank, honest, and sincere with others while keeping your words free of bias, prejudice, or malice. Candor means calling things as you see them, and not allowing your feelings to affect what you say about a person or situation.

Years ago when I was stationed at Fort Bragg, I encountered a situation that I still find hard to believe today. It all started one day during the morning formation. The platoon sergeant was talking to the soldiers about something that had gone wrong the day before, and he said something like "If you mother-_____don't get your heads out of your _____ I'm going to put all of you in jail." I just stood there in astonishment at what I was hearing. After the formation I went up to him and told him he should not have talked to the soldiers that way. He said he knew that, but they just got to him that morning. I did not fall for that excuse. I did not think he was a good leader anyway because of his military bearing and also because he just did not do the things a platoon sergeant should do.

One day, about a week later, I told him I was going to ask the commander for his job as platoon sergeant. He and I were E-7's, and neither of us had the MOS for platoon sergeant, but my DOR was higher than his, we were in the same platoon, and both of us were maintenance men. I talked to the commander and first sergeant about the job and got it. He was sent to higher headquarters and placed on the evaluation team, the place I think he wanted to be all along. I had my work cut out for me because the soldiers were having their way about things. Anyway, to make a long story short, it all worked out well for the unit as a whole. The first sergeant wanted to put me in for a Meritorious Service Medal, but I told him I did not want it because I did not think a person should get that award for working a year as a platoon sergeant. Therefore, I was given an Army Commendation Medal. I am not trying to say I was the best leader in the Army but I was one who cared about the soldiers. You do not have to be the best leader to know something is wrong and try to correct it; you just have to be a leader who cares and wants to do what is right.

Know Your Beliefs

Beliefs are assumptions or convictions you hold as true about something, a concept, or a person. They are the compass and map that guide you toward your goals and give you the surety to know you will get there. There is no more powerful directing force in human behavior than belief. To change your behavior you have to start with your beliefs. This is also true for your soldiers. Let us go back to West Germany.

In my platoon, there were two SSGs who would come to work late from time to time. I talked to each of them about being on time but that did not work. The next thing I did was to give them a counseling statement saying that the next time they were late, each would be given a summarized article 15. Because they were SSGs and each had been late before and nothing had happened, they believed lateness was ok, so they each ended up getting the so-called "dash one" or summarized article 15. I had each of them report to the unit at 04:00hours each morning for two weeks; as it happened, one of them had to sign in on Christmas morning. After that, they never came to work late again while I was the platoon sergeant. They changed their behavior because they acquired the belief that if they did not come to work on time it would affect their career, and they were right.

Beliefs are like commanders of the brain, and the brain simply does what it is told. When you say you can or cannot do something, you are right. Maybe you know someone in your unit who keeps falling out of the morning PT run; watch them and you will find that they will stop at the same place just about every time they run. The reason is they have it fixed in their minds that they cannot go any farther. If another runner runs with them they will run farther or make the complete run, because now the other runner is in control, not their mindsets. Once they are on their own again, they will go back to stopping at the same old place, because they believe they cannot make it. If you want them to make the run, just have them to run about another 50 yards. Note where they stop, add 50 yards, and tell them, "Do not worry about completing the run; all I want you to do is run up to that parking lot [or whatever the spot may be] and return to the unit." They will make the run because now they will believe they only have to go another 50 yards. They will change their belief, and their mind will tell the body to keep going up to the parking lot. After a week or so add more yardage, and before you know it those soldiers will be making the run with the unit. If you do not think your soldiers program themselves as to how far to run, the next time you have them out on the morning run, run a few blocks past the spot your run normally stops and if you look back you will find that some of your soldiers have stopped running.

Beliefs will do one or two things: they will support you, or they will limit you. If you say you think you cannot do something, you choose the one that limits you. If you say or think you can do something, you choose the one that supports you. It is your beliefs that determine how much of your potential you will be able to tap. Whenever you say, "I can't," you give your brain a command not to do something. Beliefs are like values in that they start with your environment. If all you see is failure and despair, it is very hard to make yourself believe you can become successful, but if you work on it a step at a time, you will become the leader you want to be.

You can create the belief that will allow you to be successful. That is why the Army writers write about the Battle of Gettysburg in the leadership manual, and units have boards like Audie Murphy and Sergeant York. The best way to believe you can do something is to achieve it once. That is why the soldier who maxes the PT test will do it repeatedly without practicing.

To be a successful leader you must choose your beliefs carefully. If you are convinced you are going to fail, why make an effort to try hard? The first step toward becoming a good leader is to find the beliefs that guide you to becoming one. The road to success consists of knowing the outcome you want, and taking action, seeing the results you are getting, and having the ability to change until you are successful.

What the Leader Must *Be, Know,* and *Do*

As a leader you must be a person of strong and honorable character. Your visible behavior is an implication of your character. Character is described as the sum total of an individual's inner strength and links his/her values and behavior. The leaders with strong character see clearly what they want and take action to get it. Soldiers are attracted to leaders with strong character. On the other hand, leaders with weak character are not sure of their wants; they lack the will-power, purpose, drive, and self-discipline that leaders with strong character have. A good leader has a strong character and moral values. Your soldiers will judge your character as they observe your day-to-day action, and will discern whether you are wishy-washy, lazy, selfish, or open and honest. Soldiers will entrust their lives to leaders based on their judgment of whether or not the leader has strong character traits, such as courage, candor, competence, and commitment.

> *Leaders with strong character see clearly what they want and take action to get it.*

If your character is weak your soldiers may still follow you, but only because of your rank and their sense of duty, not because you are a good leader. To increase your effectiveness in difficult crises, you and your soldiers should display traits like the following:

- Integrity
- Maturity
- Will

- Self-discipline
- Flexibility
- Confidence
- Endurance
- Decisiveness
- Coolness under stress
- Initiative
- Justice
- Self-improvement
- Assertiveness
- Empathy or compassion
- A sense of humor
- Creativity
- Bearing
- Humility and tact

To build character you must first be honest about your weaknesses and demonstrate the self-discipline on which strong and honorable character is based. To build strong and honorable character, you, as a leader, should:

- Be honest in judging the present strength of your values and character.
- Determine what values and beliefs you want to promote.
- Identify your character in relation to the mission and situations.
- Imitate other leaders who demonstrate the values, beliefs, and character you are trying to develop.

Developing character is an ongoing process; you must work hard, study, understand yourself, and exercise your willpower and self-discipline to strengthen your character. As a leader you must understand and demonstrate loyalty to the nation, the Army, and the unit. Duty, selfless-service, loyalty, and integrity are the four elements of the professional Army ethic, which is a set of principles or statements that guide professional soldiers to do the moral or right things that ought to be done. The leader who is loyal to the nation has a deep belief in servicing and defending the ideals of freedom, truth, justice, and equality. Loyalty to the Army means supporting the military and civilian chain of command, whereas loyalty to the unit means that the leader places the unit's needs and goals ahead of his/her own. It is the duty of all leaders to accept full responsibility for their soldiers' performances. They know they earn their rank and leadership positions to serve their soldiers, units, and the nation. The leaders' three general ethical responsibilities are to:

1. Be a good role model.
2. Develop their soldiers ethically.
3. Lead in such a way as to avoid putting soldiers into ethical dilemmas.

Leaders should avoid creating ethical dilemmas for soldiers that may cause them to behave unethically and result in trouble for themselves and their soldiers. Some examples of behavior that creates ethical problems are:

- Insisting on zero defects.
- Saying there is no excuse for failure.
- Maintaining a blindly can-do mindset regardless of reality.
- Not caring how a task is done, as long as it gets done.
- Covering up errors to look good to superiors.
- Telling superiors what they want to hear, rather than the truth.
- Writing reports that say what your leader wants to see, rather than the truth.
- Being loyal to those of higher rank, and not to subordinates.
- Having disrespect for those of higher rank.
- Setting goals that are impossible to attain.

True ethical dilemmas can result when two or more deeply held values collide. In such situations, using a decision-making process can help you identify the course of action that will result in the greatest moral good:

- Interpret the situation and identify the ethical dilemmas.
- Analyze the factors and forces that relate to the dilemmas.

- Choose the course of action that you believe will best serve the nation.
- Implement your course of action.

A variety of forces will influence the ethical decision-making process. Before you take action, ask yourself if you could justify the morality of your action before a group of your peers and leaders, be true to yourself and the principles for which this nation stands, and do what you believe or know is right. Some of the factors and forces that may influence your decision-making process are:

- Laws, orders, and regulations
- Basic national values
- Traditional Army values
- Institutional pressures

When faced with a situation where the right ethical choice is unclear, consider all forces and factors that relate to the situation and then select a course of action that you feel will best serve the ideals of the nation. Beware of situation ethics, which is a situation that makes you believe you should do what you know is not right, such as taking valuables from a dead soldier, or holding enemy soldiers as hostages with the hope of freeing yourself. You, as the leader, should also know about standards, because not only will you be required to enforce standards but you must also be able to meet or exceed those same standards. CTT, ARTEP, regulations, laws, LOIs, orders, and training schedules all contain standards that have to be met. Standards do not have to be easy to reach, but they must be reachable. You as the leader must be able to reach your standards as well as those of your soldiers; if not, how can you be an effective trainer and enforce that which you cannot do yourself? If your standards for your soldiers are too low, you will invite low performances; if they are too high to reach, you will create low morale among your soldiers. It is best to set high standards in stages and have your soldiers reach one stage at a time, than to have them reach for the stars all at once. You must communicate standards clearly and ensure they are understood, reachable, and that the soldiers know what to expect. If you are a leader and cannot meet standards which you expect your soldiers to reach, they will not respect you. You may be able to live with that, but eventually it will affect your career.

Years ago, one of my unit commanders was at least 40 pounds overweight, and everyone was aware of it and it was the number one IG complaint. AR 600-9 at the time stated that if a soldier was overweight, that soldier could not hold a leadership position. His boss, the LTC, knew about the weight problem but did not remove him from the leadership position. In fairness to the overweight commander, he was a good leader who made sure that the officers were trained and that the NCOs did their jobs. He also spent many hours in the gym trying to lose weight, and if there were soldiers in the unit who were overweight he would take them along. He did not like to run, but when we did he was there with us. When the time came for him to PCS, the LTC gave him a bad officer evaluation report (OER). While my commander was overweight, his boss, the LTC, was the one who was wrong because he let my commander stay in command, but when time came for my commander to PCS he was given a bad OER just in case it came back to the LTC. My commander was wrong to take the leadership position; he could have taken another position, worked on his weight problem, and still gotten a good OER. If you support your soldiers and know that they are doing wrong, do not turn around later and stab them in the back.

One of the duties of a first sergeant is to train the platoon sergeants to become first sergeant, but if the first sergeant does not know how to do his/her job, it will be very hard to train the platoon sergeants successfully. All leaders should be well trained, but junior leaders should learn as much as they can and build on it as they climb to the top, because once you get there you have to perform or risk being relieved from duty. Junior leaders are the most important of all the leaders. It's critical that their soldiers trust, respect, and are willing to follow them into combat. Let me explain.

Computer simulators are now being used to determine the senior leaders' abilities to fight and win the battle. The LTCs or whichever senior leaders are being tested go into the so-called "war room," which is no more than a room filled with computers to run the simulator.

The leaders are given computer-simulated situations in which they and their staff decide what should be done. All kinds of things come into play, such as being out of water or food, broken down supply truck, senior commander is killed, or loss of communication with higher headquarters. The simulator will win each time unless the commanders and their staff make the right choices or are familiar with the simulation. One thing the simulator cannot simulate is the feeling, morale, and skill level of the soldiers. If the computer-trained commanders and staff have to take their soldiers into combat, they are going to remember their simulator training and will try to do the same thing they did in the "war room." It is that junior leader and his or her soldiers who will have to do what the computer-trained commanders tell them, at the same time they will be on the battle-ground with their soldiers and will be able to see first-hand what is going on with the soldiers. You will be the one who knows your sol-dier got shot before the commander; it will be you who see some of them cry and call out for their mother, and it will be you whom they will depend on to get them back to their loved ones. Simulators are no more than a big video game, but the war zone is for real, and you may not get to play again.

Junior leaders are the most important of all the leaders.

Leadership Styles

The way a leader interacts directly with the soldiers is his or her style of leadership. As you read about these three styles, you will see that your values and beliefs have a great deal to do with how you lead your soldiers, and why your style is best for you. Whatever your style of leadership, it will change according to the many situations you will face, but most likely you will always come back to your style. Your leadership style will reflect your training, education, experience, environment, values, beliefs, your soldiers, and your view of the world. You can learn more about your leadership style through talking with other leaders having a similar style.

1. Directing Style of Leadership

When you tell your soldiers what you want done, how you want it done, when and where you want it done, and then supervise closely to make sure the task is done, you are using the **directing style of leadership**. This style of leadership is good when you are leading soldiers who lack experience or competence for the task. On the other hand, this style may upset a soldier who has experience and is very capable of completing the task. There will be times when only the leader may know what needs to be done and how to do it and may have to use the directing style even with experienced soldiers, yet the leader can handle the experienced soldier tactfully with success. On the battlefield the directing style will be used more than any of the other styles of leadership; however, there may not be any supervision of follow-up, the leaders know the soldiers' lives will be at stake and they may have information that they do not have time to pass on to them. The directing leadership style is mostly found in basic training units.

2. Delegating Style of Leadership

The leader is using the **delegating style of leadership** when he/she delegates problem-solving and decision-making authority to a soldier or a group of soldiers. If you delegate a task to your soldier or soldiers, be willing to take the blame should something go wrong because you are still overall responsible and accountable for their actions and performances. Some things are all right to delegate while others are not; remember, you can delegate your authority but not your responsibility. Make sure your soldiers are capable of accomplishing the task before you delegate it to them. This takes training and knowing your soldiers. Delegating authority is not a chance-taking process, and it can cause you to be relieved from duty, QMP, or perhaps reduced to a lower grade. When you receive new, inexperienced soldiers, you may start training them by using the directing style of leadership, but as time goes on and they become more competent and are motivated and share your goal, you may start supervising them less, encouraging them to ask for advice, and allowing them to participate in helping you make plans and decisions. With time, experience, and your skillful leadership, you will soon be using the delegating style with your formerly inexperienced soldiers. The delegating style of leadership is the most efficient of the three, requiring the least amount of time and energy to interact, direct, and communicate with your soldiers, but you must make sure your soldiers are well trained and responsible enough to accomplish the task. Competence is a must when delegating authority to one or more of your soldiers. This style of leadership is found throughout the Army, but it is more noticeable in personnel-type units.

3. Participating Style of Leadership

This style of leadership is one of the best ways to build your soldiers' confidence, because with this style the leader involves his/her soldiers in determining what to do and how to do it. The leader will use the **participating style of leadership** when there is time to work things out or make a decision with the soldiers. The most important things the leader must remember when using this style of leadership are that he/she is overall responsible for the quality of the plans and decisions that are made, and that he/she must maintain the final decision-making authority, which means that he/she will either make the decisions or approve those that are made by the soldiers. Having your soldiers participate is a sign of strength which they will respect you for, but most of all you will be teaching them to make decisions, which in turn will help them become better leaders themselves in the future.

Soldiers care more about working toward goals which they were involved in planning, than goals which were planned by the leader or others. If no harm will be done and time permits, it is sometimes better to say, *"We will try it your way and if it does not work we will try something else."* Notice I did not say, *"If it does not work we will try my way."* If you say it that way, the soldiers will think you want them to fail, but saying it the other way they feel they will get another chance to try, and that it is not a do-or-die situation. If their plan does not work they will still respect you for letting them try.

The leaders must be able to choose the right style of leadership at the right time for the right situation. Remember, your values and beliefs, as well as the degree of confidence you have in your soldiers, will influence the style you select.

2
Knowing and Training Your Soldiers

Putting Your Soldiers First

Y OUR NUMBER ONE CONCERN, as a leader, should be your soldiers, not yourself, your equipment, or your mission. Now before you take exception to this principle, let me ask you three questions:

1. Who operates, cleans, and takes care of your equipment?
2. Who accomplished your mission?
3. Who are the main reasons you are promoted and receive a good NCO-ER?

The answer to all three questions should be your soldiers. Without the soldiers the Army does not need you, and without them there would not be an Army. Your primary duty in the Army is the care and welfare of your soldiers. You, the leader, are their military mother and father. I do not care what type of high-tech equipment you have or how many smart bombs and computers you may use for fighting the enemy, you still need your soldiers; if you do not have any soldiers, then you are someone's else's soldier.

Leaders are promoted and get good evaluation reports because of their abilities to train and lead their soldiers. While leaders are soldiers too, when I talk about soldiers, I am talking about junior NCO and below. There are still many senior leaders who will tell you that the mission comes first before the soldiers. That reflects how they were taught early in their careers, and they may continue to teach the same thing; remember, it is not easy to change someone's beliefs. There are still leaders who say that females should not be in the Army, yet 35,000 women participated in the Gulf war of 1990-91. Those same leaders will be the first to try new uniforms, but they cannot deal with changing times. Take care of your soldiers, and they will take care of the mission when the time comes, whatever that mission may be.

Did you know that most Army equipment gets more attention than the soldiers? Think about it—soldiers will spend almost a full day or days in the motor park pulling PMCS on the equipment, compared to the amount of time senior leaders take to inspect their soldiers in the morning formation, if they do it at all. Senior leaders will go into a motor park and the first thing they will do is check fuel levels, yet they do not know whether the soldiers have food to eat. If soldiers are having problems at home or need food, most of the time they won't say anything because they think their leaders do not care, and in many units they are correct. If you want to be one of the best leaders, get promotions, good evaluation reports, and have the respect of your soldiers, make the soldiers number one on your list.

Influencing Your Soldiers

The only way you can influence your soldiers to do something is by making them want to do it. If you want them to perform well, you have to know how to talk to them and be tactful enough that they will not only want to do it but will feel good about doing it. Four of the best ways this can be done are:

1. Make them feel important.
2. Show appreciation and encouragement.
3. Become interested in your soldiers.
4. Give them what they want.

We all want to feel important, we want others to care about us, and we want to do things that show them we care. Many teens join gangs because they feel more important there than they do at home; they do not feel needed at home like they do in the gang, even though they may do things that are wrong. While Robin Hood was wrong to steal, many people liked him, so he kept on taking from the rich and giving to the poor. There are many people who will rob, steal, or even kill just to see their name in the newspaper or on the six o'clock news. Among the things that make soldiers feel important are:

- Receiving an award.
- Getting a pat on the back.
- Becoming soldier of the month, quarter, or year.
- Getting promoted.
- Getting time off.
- Conducting PT or being in charge of the run.
- Being put in charge.
- Having the best military bearing.
- Having the best display during inspection.
- Marching the section, platoon, or unit.
- Being mentioned in the unit or battalion newsletter.

Some soldiers will go all out to achieve whatever makes them feel important, and after they achieve it, they will try to accomplish the next thing that makes them feel important, or do the same thing again. They will also talk about what makes them feel important, so learn to listen to what they are saying. To many soldiers, a pat on the back or saying "thank you" means more to them than a promotion. Too many leaders will jump all over the soldiers when they do something wrong but fail to give them credit when they accomplish the right thing. Lack of appreciation is not only the reason for the breakup of some marriages but also why many soldiers go AWOL. Award your soldiers, and let them know you appreciate them; it is not as if you are giving them something for nothing.

This is what a junior NCO at Fort Hood did for his soldiers after they returned from the Gulf war. The SSG and his soldiers were scouts (tankers) for the battalion and were far ahead of the main line. When they were called back to the rear, one of the tanks threw a track so they had to stop and fix it or leave the tank behind. Knowing the enemy was in the area, they had to set up a defense and, at the same time, work on the track. They were able to get it repaired and move out of the area just in time before the enemy arrived.

Because of the situation the SSG put his soldiers in for an award but it was denied. Next, the platoon leader gave it a try, but again the awards did not go through. The SSG told the soldiers that the awards were denied, but he knew that he had to do something, so he went down to a local print shop and had some 11x14 certificates of appreciation made up. Then he took them to an artist, who drew pictures showing what each soldier was doing at the time the track was being repaired. When they were completed, he and the platoon leader signed them, and the commander presented them to the soldiers in the morning formation. I will be willing to bet you that that award meant more to those soldiers than any other award they received. That SSG in my book should have been the CSM — he knew how to influence his soldiers and how to show his appreciation of their efforts. Honest appreciation gets results where criticism and ridicule fail.

Criticism will not help you influence your soldiers. It is ineffective because it puts them on the defensive and usually makes them strive to justify themselves. It is also dangerous because it wounds their pride, hurts their sense of importance, and arouses resentment. Criticism must be done with tact to be effective. Too many senior leaders criticize junior leaders, who would feel much better if the senior leader said something like *"I remember doing that same thing when I was a _____. To correct it, I _____, and before I knew it everything was fine again."* Not only would the junior leaders feel better, but also knowing that you, a senior leader, once made the same mistake lets them feel they are on the right track. You must keep in mind that junior leaders are trying to get to where you are in your career. The way you train your leaders will most likely be the way they will train theirs, but, remember, a sorry leader will create more sorry leaders. Train junior leaders correctly and they will do the same toward their soldiers.

SGT P was one of the crew chiefs in my platoon, and he was in charge of keeping the G.P. medium tent warm for the soldiers. Whenever the platoon went on a FTX, I always had a list of things that had to be done, before, during, and after the FTX. I would assign an NCO to each task that had to be accomplished. When I placed SGT P in charge of the heater in the tent, all he had to do was have one of his soldiers place two five-gallon cans of fuel outside the tent for the heaters. During the night, if the fuel ran out, his assigned soldier or one of the guards would replace the empty can with a full one.

It was about 02:00hours that cold winter morning, as I lay there on my cot watching the flames from the heater die down. I never could sleep well in the field, maybe because I went to bed when the sun went down, but I think the real reason was because I always wanted to get my soldiers back home safely. My soldiers would see me early in the mornings talking to one of the guards or looking around the area to see if all was ok. I also knew it was my job to train my leaders to become platoon sergeant one day, and being an NCO is a day and night job. The flames from the heater got smaller and then went out. Then I called SGT P, who was sleeping about two cots over from me. When he looked up I told him that the fire was out in the heater, and he called for one of his soldiers. *"No, SGT P, I said you change the can."* Without saying another word he sat up and started getting dressed to go out in the cold to get the fuel. I could hear him outside changing the cans, and watched him as he came back inside and lit the fuel in the bottom of the heater. He pulled his cot up closer to the heater and just sat there getting warm. Later that day he asked me why I made him change the fuel cans, and I replied that when you put someone in charge of something, they are responsible for it. They can pass on that responsibility, but they are still responsible for making sure it gets done. I told him he did not make sure his soldier did the job, so I had to make sure my soldier did the job; if he didn't, the platoon leader can make me do it.

Another way to influence your soldiers is to give them what they want; if you do, you will get what you want. Every act you have performed was because you wanted something; your soldiers are the same way. As you read this book, you will find many ways to influence your soldiers.

One thing I did when I was a section chief was to get with my section after the morning formation and let them know what had to be done that day. I always had more for them to do than they normally would do in one day. I would read down my list and ask who wanted to do it, and someone would raise his or her hand and be assigned the task. They knew that when they completed the task they would be off for the rest of the day. Most of my E4's and below would be gone from about 14:00 onward each day. The junior leaders and I would stay until time to get off, and from time to time I would give one of them the rest of the day off. I was able to do that because I got more done and there was always someone around.

After an FTX, when we returned to the unit, my platoon was divided into many sections to clean and repair the field equipment. We had three days to get things back in order, so whatever part of the three days the soldiers did not use they were off. It did not matter what time we returned to the unit after we started cleaning and repairing because they knew they would be off at some point for a day and a half. The platoon leader, I (as platoon sergeant), and two or three of the junior NCOs were always there, so if something was not done or needed to be done, we did it, and when I say "we," I was included. Soldiers have great respect for leaders who do not mind getting their hands dirty, because they believe that a leader who will work with them will fight with them should they go to war.

Getting to Know Your Soldiers

To know yourself is to know what you are capable of doing; to know your leader is to know what he/she expects you to do and the support you will receive; and to know your soldiers is to know what they can and cannot do.

Knowing your soldiers is much more than the information you may have about them on a 3x5 card. it involves knowing what makes them tick, their goals, values, beliefs, and wants. The more you know about your soldiers, the better your chances will be to influence them in accomplishing the unit mission. It is important that you be aware of your soldiers' attitudes because attitudes are no more than strong beliefs or feelings toward people and situations.

Attitudes are not quick judgments; they are acquired throughout our lives and are part of our personalities. We all know that most of the time a positive attitude will result in a positive conclusion. Your soldiers' attitude about many things will not be the same as yours. For example, you may like inspecting your soldiers, but your soldiers may not like being inspected. You may like running them five miles and they may like running only two miles. To change their attitude about the inspection and get a good outcome, give them something they all like, perhaps the day off after the inspection, or you may tell them that there will be two inspections but only one if the outcome of the first one is good. You may run two miles three days or five miles one day. Once you learn to meet your soldiers halfway, you will find that you will be able to get more done and a better outcome each time. Sometimes a leader will think a soldier has a bad attitude just because he/she feels differently about a given situation. Your soldiers will shape their attitudes about you by what they see and hear. They will interpret your attitude through your behavior. Attitudes represent a powerful force in any organization. Leaders will generally encourage certain attitudes and punish others, so soldiers will tend to develop attitudes that minimize punishment and maximize rewards.

> *Your soldiers' attitudes about many things will not be the same as yours.*

Soldiers pay special attention to the behavior of their leaders. Therefore if a leader leaves the job before it is time to get off, the soldiers will soon start doing the same thing. They will develop the attitude that staying until quitting time is not important. Leaders of the unit have the greatest impact on the soldiers' attitudes. Soldiers pay more attention to what their leaders do than to what they say, so leaders must demonstrate the kind of behavior they want the soldiers to develop. All leaders are role models for soldiers, and you must always be aware of that fact. As a leader you must realize you only have control of your own attitude; you must produce an atmosphere in which they will want to change their thinking. The two most powerful ways you can lead others to adopt the attitude you wish them to have are:

1. When your soldiers perform the desired task, give them a positive reward, such as time off. This will lead them to willingly do that task in the future, knowing they will be rewarded for doing it. For example, if you want them to max the PT test, reward them.

2. Change the working conditions that surround the soldiers. Soldiers want to work with leaders who treat them with respect; they want interesting work, recognition for good work, and the chance to develop skills and get promoted. Satisfying working conditions lead to positive attitudes.

To know your soldiers is to know what they want to accomplish. If you spend as much time with your soldiers as they spend in the motor park, you will know them as well as they know the equipment. The best time to start learning about your soldiers is as soon as you or they report to the unit. When you report to a new unit the soldiers will judge you by how you dress and carry yourself. Their main concern will be whether you are able to lead them in a way that they can accomplish the unit's goals and their personal goals. If you are replacing a leader who was a good leader, they will expect you to be the same way or better; if the leader you replace was not a good leader, they will expect you to be better, but don't you feel the same way about your leaders? Soldiers do not care about a leader being hardcore as long as he/she is fair and maintains the same behavior most of the time. Do not try to be the leader you are not, because you will not be able to change overnight. If you must make adjustments, make them a little at a time.

To be a well-received leader you must be able to meet or exceed the standards set for your soldiers, and your soldiers will always expect you to out-soldier them. After reporting to a new unit, meet with the soldiers you will be in charge of. If you are a first sergeant you will want to meet with the platoon sergeants first, then the unit soldiers. If you are a platoon sergeant, the section chiefs should be your first concern. Your leaders should always be first on your list.

When meeting with your soldiers, start by letting them know what you will like to do for them, talk about time off, leaves, passes, awards, promotions, caring for the family, and other things that are important to the soldiers. Then let them know what you expect of them and ask if there are any problems. If the soldiers have another first line supervisor, let them know they should let their leader know, and to let that leader know you are there if he/she needs help; never try to take over another leader's responsibilities.

Give yourself time to find out what is going on in the unit before making a big decision. Try not to prejudge your soldiers, as they will do you. Know them for what you know about them, not based on what someone else tells you about them. The sooner you get to know your soldiers, the sooner you can start leading them in accomplishing the unit mission.

When soldiers report to your unit or section, it is important that you, the leader, provide them with all the help and assistance needed. The sponsors should be someone who will be with them each day until the in-processing is completed. Use your best soldiers for sponsors, not someone who is about to PCS even if he/she is a good soldier.

Soldiers' Values

The development of the four basic values (candor, competence, courage, and commitment) in each soldier can help strengthen the acceptance of the values of the Army ethic.

Candor is honesty and faithfulness to the truth. Team members must be able to trust one another and their leaders. Without truthfulness, this will not occur. When soldiers see their leaders or peers lying about status reports or other unit situations, they wonder if they can be trusted to be truthful in a crisis. The question arises, *"Will they be honest about wartime situations?"*

There is no time for such second-guessing in combat. **Competence** is imperative for the combat-ready team. Soldiers accept one another and their leaders when they are satisfied with their leaders' knowledge of the job and ability to apply that knowledge. Nothing deteriorates teamwork quicker than the perception that soldiers do not know how to soldier and leaders do not know how to lead. The soldiers' competence is the basis for the self-confidence critical to feeling accepted by the team.

Nothing deteriorates teamwork quicker than the perception that soldiers do not know how to soldier and leaders do not know how to lead.

Soldiers in cohesive combat-ready teams display **courage**, both moral and physical. They understand that fear in combat is natural and to be expected. Moral courage helps the combat-ready team to do the right thing in a difficult situation, even when some might strongly feel that the wrong option is more attractive. Courage on the part of one or two soldiers is contagious and becomes a way of life in the cohesive, combat-ready unit.

Commitment to the unit, the Army, and the nation occurs when soldiers accept and demonstrate the values discussed above. When soldiers willingly spend extra time to get the job done for the unit and show that unit accomplishment takes priority over personal inconvenience, they are demonstrating commitment to the unit and to the Army.

3
What Is NCO-ER Leadership?

NCO-ER leadership is the ability of the rated NCO to successfully meet or exceed the leadership standards set by the Army and the rating officials. In other words, NCO-ER leadership is the ability of the rated NCO to earn a successful or excellent NCO-ER. As I said in Chapter 1, "No matter how good a leader you are, or think you are, unless your rating officials state it on your NCO-ER, you are just another NCO in the Army," as far as the Army is concerned. The primary goal of the rating official is to evaluate your leadership accomplishments during the rating period. Do you remember, in Chapter 1, the list of things that the Army expects you to do? That list is broken down into ten parts which the rating officials will use when completing your report (NCO-ER), which will be sent to the Department of the Army (DA). They in turn will use the report to see how you measure up with other NCOs in your MOS and rank for promotion, assignments, schooling, and retention in the Army.

NCO Values and Responsibilities

NCO values and responsibilities that are listed on the NCO-ER are:

- Values
- Competence
- Physical Fitness
- Military Bearing
- Leadership
- Training
- Responsibility and Accountability

The rater will indicate the level of performance (Excellence, Success, or Need Improvement) for each responsibility by placing a type-written or handwritten "X" in the appropriate box, except for part IV (a). For the seven comments concerning values, the rater will place an "X" in the "YES" or "NO" box for each comment. For all the other responsibilities, the rater will place an "X" in the "Excellence," "Success," or "Need Improvement" box. Definitions of performance levels are as follows:

- **Excellence:** Exceeds standards; demonstrated by specific examples and measurable results, special and unusual; achieved by only a few; clearly better than most other NCOs.
- **Success:** Meets all standards. Majority of ratings are in this category, fully competitive for schooling and promotion. The goal of counseling is to bring all NCOs to this level.
- **Need Improvement:** Missed meeting some standards.

Specific bullet examples are mandatory for Excellence or Need Improvement ratings; more on this later. Now let us look and see how that long list of things the Army expects you to do is broken down into ten parts and at the same time what you can do to receive that Success or Excellence NCO-ER.

Part One
Army Values

One of the most important changes that were made on the NCO-ER was Army Values. Because the Army has made a big issue of the seven values, it is important that you get a "YES" in all seven blocks. Let us look and see what you need to do.

1. **LOYALTY:** When you talk about loyalty, you are talking about faithfulness, devotion, dedication, patriotism, duty, honor, reliability, dependability, and trustworthiness. Loyalty is commitment, which makes your soldiers feel good about going into a combat zone with you. Your loyalty gives your soldiers faith that they will return home to their loved ones. The loyalty of your soldiers is a gift they give to you, and you should give them that same gift. If you are a faithful, dependable, and trustworthy person, that is loyalty. It is hard to get a "NO" in the loyalty box, as it covers so much. During your counseling for your report, make sure your rater tells you what he/she expects concerning loyalty. Ask yourself these questions:

   - Am I dedicated to my soldiers, Army, and duty?
   - Can my soldiers, peers, and others depend on me?
   - Do I observe priorities from higher headquarters?
   - Do I work within the system without manipulating it for personal gains?

2. **DUTY:** Duty begins with everything required of you by law, regulation, and orders. It is fulfilling your obligation, and not trying to get another NCO to fulfill it. It is taking full responsibility for your actions as well as the actions of your soldiers. Duty is responsibility, trust, obligation, and sometimes burden. Duty means accomplishing all assigned tasks to the fullest of your ability. A duty is a legal or moral obligation to do what needs to be done without being told to do it. Ask yourself:

- Do I fulfill my obligations—professional, legal, and moral?
- Do I carry out the mission requirements?
- Do I meet professional standards?
- Do I set the example?
- Do I comply with policies and directives?
- Do I continually pursue excellence?

3. **RESPECT:** In the Army respect means recognizing and appreciating the inherent dignity and worth of all people. You must foster a climate in which you treat everyone with dignity and respect regardless of race, gender, creed, or religious beliefs. Respect includes the way people treat each other and those they meet. When you salute officers whom you do not know or never have seen before, it is out of respect for their rank that you salute them; on the other hand, if you do not salute them, you are being disrespectful. Remember, your soldiers will do what they see you do. You must have respect for your soldiers; you do not have to like what they like or do what they do, but you show respect for them by not putting down what they do or say. Now ask yourself:

   - Do I treat people as they should be treated?
   - Do I create a climate of fairness and equal opportunity?
   - Am I discreet and tactful when correcting or questioning others?
   - Do I show concern for, and make an effort to check on, the safety and well being of others?
   - Am I courteous?
   - Do I take advantage of my position of authority or rank?

4. **SELFLESS-SERVICE:** Selfless-service does not mean that you cannot have a strong ego, high self-esteem, or even healthy ambition. Rather, selfless-service means that you do not make decisions or take actions just to help your career or image. Your duty as an NCO is to train, lead, and care for the soldiers; if you do that without thinking about promotion, schooling, or assignment, you will be a selfless leader. On top of that, you will most likely get all the

things you want even faster, because your training, caring, and leadership will be noted on your NCO-ER by your rater and senior rater. Selfless-service means doing what is right for the nation, the Army, and your organization and soldiers. It means putting these responsibilities above your own interest. This does not mean you neglect your family or yourself. It means you should learn how to balance the two and, at the same time, know that the nation and the Army come first. When thinking about selfless-service, ask yourself these questions:

- Do I put the welfare of the nation, the Army, and soldiers before my own?
- Do I sustain team morale?
- Do I share the soldiers' hardships?
- Do I give the soldiers credit for their success, or do I claim it?
- Do I accept responsibility for failure?
- Do I try to put on a show in front of my leader?
- Is my leadership self-motivated?

5. **HONOR:** The expression "honorable person" describes those people who live such that their words and deeds are above re-proach; it refers to both the character traits an individual actually possesses and which are recognized and respected. Honor means demonstrating an understanding of what is right and taking pride in the community's acknowledgment of that reputation. Living honorably strengthens Army values, not only for you, but for oth-ers as well. To be an honorable person, you must be true to your oath and live Army values in all you do. For an Army leader, honor means putting the Army values above self-preservation; this is es-sential for creating a bond of trust among members of the Army and between the Army and the nation it serves. Honor is living up to all the Army values, which is what you promised to do when you took your oath of office or enlistment. Ask yourself these ques-tions concerning honor:

- Do I live up to the Army values?
- Do I lie, cheat, steal, or tolerate those actions by others?

- Am I true to my word?
- Is self-preservation my goal?

6. **INTEGRITY:** Integrity is doing what is right—legally and morally. It also means goodness, honesty, uprightness, virtue, and decency. Having integrity means being both morally complete and true to oneself. People of integrity consistently act according to principle, not just what might work at the moment. Your personal values may and probably do extend beyond the Army values to include political, cultural, or religious beliefs.

   Leaders of integrity make their principles known, and consistently act accordance with them. If you knew for a fact that your ISG is doing drugs or selling them and one day the CID comes to the unit and asked you if you think your ISG is taking or selling drugs, what would you do or say, and would you do anything before the CID came? If one of the sergeants was having sex with one of the female soldiers and you walked in and caught them in the act, what would you do? What if you and some of the other sergeants went TDY and were given an Army charge card, and one of the sergeants asked you to put a charge on your card to get something for his wife, and he would give you the money back on payday, what would you do? Remember, integrity is doing what is right. Here are more questions to ask yourself concerning integrity:

   - Do I do what is right legally and morally?
   - Do I possess high personal moral standards?
   - Am I honest in word and deed?
   - Do I show consistently good moral judgment and behavior?
   - Do I put what is right ahead of being popular?

7. **PERSONAL COURAGE:** Personal Courage is facing fear, danger, or adversity (physical or moral). It is not the absence of fear; rather, it is the ability to put fear aside and do what is necessary. It takes two forms—physical and moral. Physical courage means overcoming fear of bodily harm and doing your duty. Moral courage is the willingness to stand firm on your values, principles, and

convictions, even when things go wrong. Moral courage is essential to living the Army values of integrity and honor every day; it often expresses itself as candor. In combat, physical and moral courage may blend. The right thing to do may not only be unpopular but dangerous as well.

If one of your female soldiers came to you and said that a unit leader asked to have sex with her, and that he would make sure that she gets the next stripe for promotion, what would you do? Ask yourself these questions concerning personal courage?

- Do I show physical and moral bravery?
- Do I take responsibility for decisions and actions?
- Do I accept responsibility for mistakes and shortcomings?

Part Two
Competence

Competence, the know-how or having the right stuff, is the leader's ability to do things. Competence works hand in hand with confidence. To become competent you first must have confidence in whatever you become competent in doing. As a leader you must have:

- Competence in yourself
- Competence in your soldiers
- Competence in your job
- Competence in your unit
- Competence in the Army values

Competence in yourself: Know yourself so that you can maximize your strengths and work hard to improve your weaknesses. As a leader, you must realize you are three people in one, which are:

1. Who you are
2. Who you think you are
3. Who others think you are

Remember, no matter who you are or think you are, it is who your rater and senior rater think you are that counts. Ask your seniors, peers, and soldiers if they can give you honest feedback about yourself; if you take their feedback to heart and try to improve (needed or not), you have a foundation for knowing yourself, your job, and your soldiers. To know yourself is knowing the conditions that bring out the good and bad in you at the same time, encouraging the good, suppressing the bad, and directing that good behavior toward accomplishing the unit's mission. You must also exercise self-discipline to bring out the good and suppress the bad in your soldiers.

To be competent, you must be able to communicate effectively so that your soldiers understand exactly what you are trying to tell them. You communicate to direct, influence, coordinate, encourage, supervise, train, coach, and think through a problem and translate that idea in a clear, concise, measured fashion. To help your soldiers live according to Army values, you must know why Army values are important and how to apply them to everyday Army life.

Competence in your soldiers: It will take a long time to get to know your soldiers, and some of them you will never get to know, because they may be:

- TDY
- Working as a driver
- Working in another unit
- Working at one of the rangers
- Working in supply or the mess hall

There will be other soldiers who will work side by side with you day after day and you will still not get to know them. Soon as you get to know some soldiers, they will PCS and you will get new ones. As a leader, your number one concern should be your soldiers, not yourself, your equipment, or the unit's mission.

Now before you get all upset and throw this book into the trashcan, let me explain why I say your soldiers should be your number one concern. As a leader you are paid to accomplish the Army's mission, whatever that mission may be, and most of the time you will need your soldiers to accomplish that mission. You get promoted and receive a good assignment and evaluation report because of your ability to train and lead your soldiers. You can have all the equipment and knowledge you want, but without the soldiers, nine out of ten times the mission will not be accomplished.

If you spend as much time with your soldiers as some leaders spend in the motor pool looking at dead line equipment, not only will you have better soldiers, but you will also receive better NCO-ERs that will get you promotions and good assignments. You must never forget that you are responsible for your soldiers' performance and accountable for their actions. As a leader you must:

- Train your soldiers in peacetime, as they will fight in combat.
- Prepare your soldiers for the fears of battle.
- Keep your soldiers active and thinking about the mission.
- Not push your soldiers unnecessarily.
- Keep your soldiers informed.

Competence in your job: In today's Army, most jobs require technical and tactical skills and knowledge. Technical knowledge is knowledge required to perform all tasks and functions related to your position, including the ability to operate and maintain all assigned equipment. You must strive to learn how to use your equipment in the most effective manner to support the accomplishment of your mission. To obtain the technical knowledge you need, study and work hard in school and in your unit. Do not be afraid to ask your seniors, peers, and soldiers to help you learn. If you are incompetent on a particular system, admit it and take immediate action to correct the deficiency. Technical skills require you to:

- Possess or develop the expertise necessary to accomplish all assigned tasks and functions.
- Know the standards for task accomplishments.
- Know the small unit tactics, techniques, and procedures that support the organization's mission.
- Know the drills that support the organization's mission.
- Prepare clear, concise operation orders.

- Understand how to apply the factors of mission, enemy, terrain, and weather, troops' time available, and civil considerations (METF-TC) to mission analysis.
- Master basic soldier's skills.
- Know how to use and maintain equipment.

Tactical knowledge is the ability to employ your soldiers and their equipment. The Army recognizes nine principles of war. You must understand them and consider their applicability to your situation. The nine principles of war are:

1. Objective	4. Economy of force	7. Security
2. Offensive	5. Maneuver	8. Simplicity
3. Mass	6. Surprise	9. Unity of command

Your tactical knowledge will not be complete unless you also understand the doctrine and tactics of potential enemies. Tactical skills require you to:

- Know how to apply war-fighting doctrine within the commander's intent.
- Apply your professional knowledge, judgment, and war-fighting skills at the appropriate leadership level.
- Combine and apply skills with people, ideas, and things to accomplish short-term missions.
- Apply skills with people, ideas, and things to train for, plan, prepare, execute, and assess offensive, defensive stability, and support actions.

Competence in your unit: You as the leader must know your unit's limitations and capabilities. The forces that drive a disciplined unit come from within that unit. These forces are the values, character, and will of the leader and soldiers. A unit's character reflects the character of its leaders and soldiers. As a leader, you must have self-discipline, which means you must force yourself to do your duty regardless of stress, exhaustion, or other conditions. A disciplined unit forces itself to do its duty in every situation. In a disciplined unit soldiers have the self-confidence and initiative needed to take decisive action, while at the same time helping the unit accomplish the mission. Your soldiers will take pride in being members of a unit having disciplined proficiency.

Disciplined proficiency is more than just competency. It comes from realistic training and cross-training, and from leaders who care enough to coach and teach their soldiers. It occurs when soldiers are so proficient and motivated that they want to focus all their energy on the mission. They willingly give of themselves to make the unit better. Caring is essential to the soldiers and the unit. A soldier's belief that his/her leaders and friends care for him/her and will always do their best to help him/her increases the desire to fight to protect his/her fellow soldiers. In a unit that produces good soldiers, a leader:

- Does not continually reassign soldiers and junior leaders to different jobs and squads just because one squad temporarily has fewer members than the other squads.
- Does not continually reassign drivers, because they may not take pride in their vehicles.
- Does not rotate experienced soldiers into "softer" jobs as a reward for good service.
- Puts soldiers through tough and realistic training that requires them to do things that they do not believe they can do as individuals or as a unit; as they go through the training, they must help each other learn and develop.
- Resolves interpersonal conflicts to restore respect, confidence, and candid communication between soldiers. Broken bonds between unit members cause the unit to deteriorate and become unable to function under stress.
- Makes garrison training interesting and as realistic as possible so that soldiers train as they will fight in combat, and training does not become tiresome and destroy morale.
- Keeps unit members working as a team toward a common purpose that supports the mission.

Unit cohesiveness is an important factor in peacetime and in combat. Cohesive units under good leadership will work together to ensure that training is properly planned, executed, and assessed with the objective of maintaining the highest possible readiness standards. Unit cohesion cannot be developed and maintained without strong leadership, and small-unit leadership is the key.

You as a leader must learn how to make a group of ordinary soldiers into an extraordinary team, which in turn will produce an outstanding unit.

Competence in the Army Values: Values are your personal, private, and individual beliefs about what is most important to you. Values govern your entire lifestyle, the food you eat, and even how you raise your children or lead your soldiers. Your values will also influence your priorities and decisions. Values are principles, morals, ideals, standards, ethics, beliefs, and what is important to you. With that in mind, the Army values are what's important to the Army and should be important to you as a leader. The Army values are one of the areas your rater and senior rater will rate you in, and are the values you are expected to teach your soldiers. Below is a list of the seven Army values and what you and your soldiers should be doing concerning each.

1. LOYALTY
- Bear true faith and allegiance in the correct order to the Constitution, the Army, and the organization.
- Observe the priorities of higher headquarters.
- Work within the system without manipulating it for personal gain.

2. DUTY
- Fulfill obligations – professional, legal, and moral.
- Carry out mission requirements.
- Meet professional standards.
- Set the example.
- Comply with policies and directives.
- Continually pursue excellence.

3. RESPECT

- Treat people as they should be treated.
- Create a climate of fairness and equal opportunity.
- Be discreet and tactful when correcting or questioning others.
- Show concern for, and make an effort to check on, the safety and well being of others.
- Be courteous.
- Do not take advantage of positions of authority.

4. SELFLESS-SERVICE

- Put the welfare of the nation, the Army, and soldiers before your own.
- Sustain team morale.
- Share soldiers' hardships.
- Give credit for success to others and accept responsibility for failure.

5. HONOR

- Live up to the Army values.
- Do not lie, cheat, steal, or tolerate those actions in others.

6. INTEGRITY

- Do what is right, legally and morally.
- Possess high personal moral standards.
- Be honest in word and deed.
- Show consistently good moral judgment and behavior.
- Put being right ahead of being popular.

7. PERSONAL COURAGE

- Show physical and moral bravery.
- Take responsibility for decisions and actions.
- Accept responsibility for mistakes and shortcomings.

Part Three
Physical Fitness and Military Bearing

Physical Fitness

Physically fit soldiers outperform unfit soldiers two to one, and are what is needed in the Army today and in the future. Physically fit leaders are better able to think, decide, and act appropriately under pressure. Soldiers who are physically fit feel more competent and confident, and they can handle stress better, work longer and harder, and recover faster than those who are less fit or unfit

The physical demands of leadership positions, prolonged deployments, and continuous operations can erode more than just physical attributes. Soldiers are deployed more often than before, which is one reason why they should maintain a very high level of fitness during deployment and demanding operations. If your soldiers are not physically fit, the effects of additional stress snowball until their mental and emotional fitness are compromised as well.

Maintaining physical fitness is an ethical as well as a practical imperative. Physically fit soldiers and leaders are the beginning of unit readiness. Combat drains soldiers physically, mentally, and emotionally. To minimize those effects, Army leaders and soldiers must be physically fit.

The Army Physical Fitness Test (APFT) measures a baseline level of physical fitness. Fitness programs that emphasize training specifically for the APFT are boring and do not prepare soldiers for the varied stresses of combat, so you must make every effort to design a physical fitness program that prepares your soldiers for what you expect them to do in combat.

Military Bearing

As a leader, you are expected to look like a soldier, while wearing your uniform at all times. A big part of military bearing is being within the guidelines of the height and weight program, and displaying military courtesy and appearance. You must have the "I am proud of my uniform, my unit, and myself" attitude. As an Army leader, your emotional attributes of self-control, balance, and stability contribute to how you feel and therefore to how you interact with others. Leaders who are emotionally mature also have a better awareness of their own strengths and weaknesses. Leaders must also have self-control and must be able to control their emotions. This encourages feedback from your soldiers that can expand your sense of what is really going on. Military bearing is the way you carry yourself as a soldier on or off duty, state-side or overseas. Your standards for the military should be very high, whether you are a private or a command sergeant major. The way you sit, talk, and walk are all a part of your military bearing. The military bearing that is most noticeable by your superiors and other soldiers are:

- The way you wear your uniform.
- How well groomed you are.
- Your attitude toward other soldiers and officers.

The way you wear your uniform tells a great deal about your personality. To learn more about wearing the male and female uniforms, read AR 670-1. This will explain such things as:

- How to wear the uniform.
- When and where to wear uniforms.
- What items you can wear on uniforms.
- The type of shoes and boots to wear with the uniforms.
- Head gear, how and when to wear it.
- Special skills, marksmanship, and ID badges.
- Rank insignia and brassards.
- U.S. Army tapes and nametags.
- Belts, gloves, sweaters, windbreakers, and medals.
- Haircuts, mustaches, and sideburns.
- What rings to wear and how many.
- Fingernails and lipstick.
- Make-up, chains, hair color, wigs, and much more.

Part Four
Mental and Physical Toughness

Mental Toughness

Mental toughness comes from your will, self-discipline, initiative, judgment, self-confidence, intelligence, and cultural awareness.

Will: The will of a soldier is more important than his/her weapon. It is the inner drive that compels soldiers and leaders to keep going when they are exhausted, hungry, afraid, cold and wet, or when it would be easier to quit. Will without competence is useless; it is not enough that soldiers are willing, or even eager, to fight. They must know how to fight. It is easy to talk about will when things go well, but the best test of your will comes when things go badly, when events seem to be out of control, when you think your boss has forgotten you, or when the plan does not seem to work and it looks like you are going to lose. It is then that you must draw on your inner reserves to persevere to do your job to the maximum of your ability, and then to remain faithful to your soldiers, your unit, and your country.

Self-discipline: Self-disciplined soldiers are masters of their impulses – a mastery that comes from the habit of doing the right thing. Self-discipline allows the Army leaders to do the right thing regardless of the consequences for them and their soldiers. During peacetime, self-discipline is why you take the unit out for a hard training – for example, when it is raining or is cold outside. It is what makes a soldier keep training to pass the PT test, or keep going to the range to become an expert with his/her weapon. It is what keeps a soldier in school after duty hours or drives another soldier to keep studying for the soldier-of-the-month award or the promotion board. Self-discipline does not mean that you never get tired or discouraged; it means that you do what needs to be done regardless of your feelings.

Initiative: Soldiers who possess initiative have the ability to be self-starters, to act when there are no clear instructions, to act when the situation changes or when the plan falls apart. Initiative drives the Army leaders to seek a better method, to anticipate what must be done, and to perform without waiting for instructions. To read and learn more about initiative, see:

- FM 100-5 - Discusses initiative as it relates to military actions at the operational level.
- FM 100-34 - Discusses the relationship of initiative to command and control.
- FM 100-40 - Discusses initiative in the art of tactics.
- FM 22-100 - Discusses building teams and commander's intent, as well as development of soldiers.

Your leadership style and the unit climate you establish can either encourage or discourage initiative; you can instill initiative in your soldiers or drive it out. If you set a "zero defects" standard, you risk strangling initiative.

Judgment: This is the ability to size up a situation quickly, determine what is important, and decide what needs to be done. However, you do need to think through the consequences of what you are about to do before you take action. Some factors that aid judgment are:

- The boss's intent
- The desired goal
- Rules and laws
- Regulations, experience, and values

Good judgment also includes the ability to size up your soldiers, peers, and the enemy for strengths, weaknesses, and potential actions. Judgment and initiative go hand in hand. As an Army leader, you must weigh what you know and make decisions in situations where others do nothing. Judgment is something that you must instill in your soldiers.

Self-confidence: This is the faith that you will act correctly and properly in any situation, even one in which you are under stress and do not have all the information you want. Competence is what leads to self-confidence; it is based on mastering skills, which takes hard work and dedication. Do not mistake bragging, bluster, or self-promotion for self-confidence. Truly self-confident leaders do not need to advertise; their actions say it all. Soldiers want leaders who understand the situation, know what needs to be done, and demonstrate that understanding and knowledge. Self-confident leaders instill self-confidence in their soldiers. Along with will and self-discipline, self-confidence helps leaders act or do what must be done in circumstances where it would be easier to do nothing, and at the same time convince their soldiers to act as well.

Intelligence: Leaders think, learn, and reflect, then apply what they learned. All soldiers have some intellectual ability that, when developed, allows them to analyze and understand a situation. Although some soldiers are smarter than others, all soldiers can develop the capabilities they have. When things do not go quite the way they intended, intelligent leaders are confident enough to step back and ask, "Why did things turn out that way?" Then they are smart enough to build on their strengths and avoid making the same mistake again.

Cultural Awareness: Culture is a set of beliefs, values, and assumptions about what is important, shared by a group. Within the Army, soldiers come from widely different backgrounds; their schooling, race, gender, and religion as well as a host of other factors influence and shape them. Although they share Army values, an African-American soldier from rural Texas may look at many things differently from, say, a third-generation Irish-American soldier who grew up in Philadelphia or a Native American from the Pacific Northwest. Army leaders not only recognize that people are different; they value them because of their differences, because they are soldiers. As an Army leader your job is not to make everyone the same; instead, your job is to take advantage of those differences and build a cohesive team. There is great religious, ethnic, and social diversity in the Army, and soldiers of different backgrounds bring different talents to the table. By joining the Army, these soldiers have agreed to adopt the Army culture. Army leaders make this easier by embracing and making use of everyone's talents. What's more, they create a team where soldiers know they are valuable and their talents are important.

Physical Toughness

Physical toughness is everything you do to maintain good health. A soldier unable to fight because of dysentery is as much a loss as one who is wounded. Healthy soldiers can perform under extremes in temperature, humidity, and other conditions better than unhealthy ones. Physical toughness also includes avoiding whatever degrades your health, such as substance abuse, obesity, and smoking.

Because of the need for highly physically fit soldiers, the Army is looking at ways to make the PT test tougher. Soldiers will still do the push-ups, sit-ups, and two-mile run, but there are new standards set for age and gender. The 300-point scoring system will be retained, and the minimum passing score will still be 60 points for each event, and 180 for the entire test. The tougher PT standards will:

1. Require men and women to do the same number of push-ups, but relax the number of repetitions required to max the push-ups portion of the test.
2. Require all soldiers, except those 26 years old and older, to run faster minimum times in the two-mile run.
3. Establish three new age groups for older soldiers, which are presently 52-56, 57-61, and 62 plus.

The commander and supervisors will monitor all soldiers of their command to insure that they maintain the proper weight, body composition, and personal appearance. At a minimum, soldiers will be weighed when they take the Army Physical Fitness Test or at least every six months. Soldiers who are overweight (including pregnant soldiers) will:

- Be considered non-promotable.
- Not be authorized to attend professional or civilian schooling.

- Not be assigned to a command position.
- Not be able to reenlist or extend their enlistment.

In many cases fitness begins with weight reduction. Aerobic fitness is related to a soldier's body fat; the higher the percentage of fat, the less likely the soldier is to be aerobically fit and the harder it is to maintain a higher level of physical stamina and endurance.

Soldiers who are not overweight are less likely to develop heart disease, high blood pressure, and diabetes. To maintain the proper weight, they need to obtain the proper nutrition and exercise regularly. Physical toughness also deals with cracking down on drug use in the military, such as marijuana, cocaine, met amphetamine, and ecstasy. During the Department of Defense crackdown on drug use in the military, the Pentagon increased random drug testing and standardized punishment for drug users in the Army. The goal is to ensure that regular random testing is done in a way that serves as a deterrent as well as a detection method. Most of the soldiers who test positive for these drugs are in the 18-26 age group.

Leaders who are physically fit and have good military bearing:

- Are better able to think and decide under pressure.
- Handle stress better, work harder and longer, and recover faster.
- Maintain a very high level of fitness.
- Design fitness programs that prepare soldiers for combat.
- Are within the guidelines of the height and weight programs.
- Display military courtesy and appearance.
- Are proud of their uniform and unit.
- Are emotionally mature, aware of their strengths and weaknesses.
- Have self-control and maintain good health.
- Have a good attitude toward other soldiers and officers.
- Are masters of their impulses.
- Do what needs to be done, regardless of their feelings.
- Seek a better method, anticipate what must be done.
- Have the ability to size up a situation quickly.
- Build on strengths and avoid making the same mistakes.

Part Five
Leadership

Mission First

It is not easy being an Army leader. The old saying that actions speak louder than words has never been more true than with today's NCOs. You must embrace Army values and teach them to your soldiers. Remember, you must always put your soldiers first in order to accomplish the Army's mission, which means you must master the tactical skills for your unit.

Tactical skills include tactics appropriate to your grade level of responsibility as well as those of your soldiers. You should not be satisfied with just doing what would get your organization through today; you must be concerned about what it will need tomorrow. You must strive to master your job, your soldiers' jobs, and at the same time be prepared to take over your boss's job. As you learn all of those jobs of increasing responsibilities, you will face new equipment, new ideas, and new ways of thinking and doing things.

You must learn to apply all these skills to accomplish the Army's mission. Army schools teach you the basic job skills, but you will learn even more at the unit or job site, at which time you should add to your job knowledge and skills. As you master your job and those of your soldiers, you will then be able to accomplish the Army's mission because at that time you will know not only what you can do but what your soldiers can do as well.

Genuine Concern for Your Soldiers

To get a good rating in part IV (d) "Leadership" on your NCO-ER, you must show genuine concern for your soldiers. For more in-depth information about your soldiers, read Chapter 2 again. Genuine concern for your soldiers means creating an environment in which they can learn and grow. It means holding them to high standards, but at the same time ensuring those standards can be reached. You must teach them to do their jobs so they can function in peacetime and win in combat. You show concern for your soldiers when you treat them equally, fairly, and with respect.

The number one reason you are in charge of soldiers is to train them to fight and win in combat, and return home to their loved ones. Refuse to cut corners, share their hardships, and set an example for them to follow. Genuine concern for your soldiers means providing them with family support which assures them that their families will be taken care of, whether the soldiers are home or deployed, and that there is a family support group in place if needed.

Genuine concern for your soldiers means demanding that they do their duty, even at the risk of their lives in combat. You must train them, and the training must be rigorous and as realistic as possible; they must train as they will fight in combat, which means you must be very creative.

Instilling the Spirit to Achieve and Win

The true measure of leadership is influence – nothing more, nothing less. To instill the spirit to achieve and win, you must influence and motivate your soldiers so they will be able to accomplish the Army's mission. You as an NCO have the power to influence the beliefs and values of your soldiers by setting the example. You must train your soldiers as you want them to fight, by using tough training. Tough training does not mean training in which the leader hazes or yells at the soldiers in an effort to cause artificial stress. Tough training conducted to standards will teach your soldiers to do things as individuals and as a team that they did not believe possible. It will give your soldiers confidence in themselves, in each other, and in you. No training can be accomplished unless you can influence your soldiers. Leaders who influence:

- Use appropriate methods to reach goals while operating and improving.
- Motivate soldiers to accomplish assigned tasks and missions.
- Set the example by demonstrating enthusiasm for, and if necessary methods of, accomplishing assigned tasks.

- Make themselves available to assist peers and soldiers.
- Share information with soldiers.
- Encourage soldiers and peers to express candid opinions.
- Actively listen to feedback and act appropriately based on it.
- Mediate peer conflicts and disagreements.
- Tactfully confront and correct others when necessary.
- Earn respect and obtain the willing cooperation of peers, soldiers, and superiors.
- Challenge others to match their examples.
- Know how and what to inspect.
- Use technology, especially information technology, to enhance communications.
- Take care of soldiers and their families, providing for their health, welfare, morale, and training.
- Are persuasive in peer discussions and prudently rally peer pressure against peers when required.
- Provide a team vision for the future.
- Shape the organizational climate by setting, sustaining, and ensuring a values-based environment.

Motivation is the cause of action. It gives your soldiers the will to do what must be done to accomplish the Army's mission. All your soldiers need to do to be sincerely motivated is to have confidence in themselves, each other, the unit, and you, and support the cause. Training them to fight and win as a cohesive, disciplined team will have a valuable motivational effect. You must keep a broad point of view on human nature and motivation. Do not allow yourself to hold the narrow view that soldiers are only motivated by fear of their leaders. You can motivate your soldiers by:

- Inspiring, encouraging, and guiding them toward mission accomplishment.
- Not showing discouragement when facing setbacks.
- Attempting to satisfy soldiers' needs.
- Giving soldiers the reason for assigned tasks.
- Providing accurate, timely, and (when appropriate) positive feedback.
- Actively listening to feedback from them.

- Using feedback to modify duties, tasks, requirements, and goals when appropriate.
- Recognizing individual and team accomplishments and rewarding them appropriately.
- Justly applying disciplinary measures.
- Keeping them informed; letting them know what is going on.
- Clearly articulating expectations.
- Considering duty position, capabilities, and developmental needs when assigning tasks.
- Providing early warning to their leaders of tasks they will be responsible for.
- Defining requirements by issuing clear and concise orders or guidance.
- Allocating as much time as needed for task completion.
- Accepting responsibility for organizational performance.
- Crediting them for good performance.
- Taking responsibility for and correcting poor performance.

Your job as a leader goes beyond teaching your soldiers how to fight and survive; you must also teach them the "winning spirit" or "warrior spirit," which is the ability to forge victory out of the chaos of battle and to overcome fear, hunger, deprivation, and fatigue. As a leader, your ability to instill this will in your soldiers starts with examples you set, the attitudes you express, the expectations you establish, and the standards you enforce.

Setting the Example – *Be*, *Know*, and *Do*

BE, KNOW, and DO clearly and concisely state the characteristics of an Army leader, which underline everything a leader does, including adopting and living Army values. Being a leader in today's Army is not easy; however, the tools are available to every leader, and it is up to you to take advantage of them. Your soldiers are used to certain creature comforts, such as being fed, warm, dry, and safe. They will depend on you to take care of them. The chart below gives some examples of what a leader must BE, KNOW, and DO.

Be

BE a person of strong and honorable character by:
- Using determination
- Using compassion
- Using self-discipline
- Being a role model
- Taking initiative
- Being flexible
- Being consistent

BE committed to the professional Army ethic by:
- Being loyal to the nation, Army, and your unit
- Being a master of selfless-service
- Having integrity
- Performing your duty or duties to the best of your abilities

BE an example of individual values by:
- Having courage
- Being candor
- Being competent
- Being committed

BE able to resolve complex ethical dilemmas by:
- Interpreting the situation
- Analyzing all facts and forces that apply
- Choosing a course of action that seems best for the nation

Know

KNOW the four factors of leadership and how they affect each other by:
- Knowing your leaders
- Knowing the situation
- Knowing your soldiers
- Knowing your means of communication

KNOW standards by:
- Knowing the sources of Army standards
- Knowing how standards relate to combat

KNOW yourself by:
- Knowing your personality and performance
- Knowing your strengths and weaknesses
- Knowing your skills, attitudes, and knowledge

KNOW human nature by:
- Knowing your soldiers and their potential for good and bad behavior
- Knowing how depression and sadness contribute to fear and panic, and how fear affects performance

KNOW your job by:
- Planning and communicating effectively
- Supervising, teaching, coaching, and counseling
- Displaying technical and tactical competence
- Developing soldiers
- Making good decisions that your soldiers will accept
- Using available systems

KNOW your unit by:
- Knowing your unit's capabilities and limitations

Do

DO provide purpose by:
- Explaining the "WHY" of the mission
- Communicating your intent

DO provide direction by:
- Planning, setting goals, and maintaining standards
- Making decisions and solving problems
- Supervising, evaluating, teaching, coaching, and counseling
- Training soldiers and soldier teams

DO provide motivation by:

- Taking care of your soldiers
- Serving as the ethical standard bearer
- Developing cohesive soldier teams
- Making soldiering meaningful
- Rewarding performance that exceeds standards
- Correcting performance not meeting standards
- Punishing soldiers who intentionally fail to meet standards or follow orders

Part Six
Training

Individual Training

Initially, the new soldiers are concerned about fitting in and belonging. They want a place on the team, but are not sure how others will accept them. All soldiers experience this adjustment when they enter the Army and learn to live with others from many different backgrounds. They go through a process of checking out other soldiers and leaders. The more they get to know them, the more they realize how much they have in common and the more comfortable they feel with them. Soldiers adjust to their new unit differently. Some "come on strong," bragging about past exploits or telling "war stories" from past Army experiences; others adjust by withdrawing and watching quietly until they begin to trust fellow soldiers in the unit. Some adjust quickly, while others fit in more slowly. A few may need help from the leader, and occasionally a soldier is not able to adjust to the team at all. All soldiers, however, go through some concern about whether or not they belong to the unit.

During peacetime training, soldiers learn technical and tactical skills and have time to apply them to unit operations. During combat, they bring these skills when they join the unit, but have to learn their application in the specific unit and battle environment. The quicker soldiers learn specific techniques, the quicker they will be accepted as team members. It is very important that soldiers be well trained in their MOS.

One fear soldiers have is that they will somehow cause serious injury or death to other soldiers. They also fear being wounded or killed. All the dynamics of being in a new unit cause stress on soldiers. The leader and other soldiers can help them find ways to cope with the stress; the key is that they deal with stress in some manner. (FM 26-2 provides information on dealing with stress.) The leader plays a key role in the individual soldier training. He/she realizes that team building can be, and must be, made to work in any environment, and that he/she must follow the basic principles, which are:

- Know the job
- Know the soldier
- Develop the soldier
- Structure the situation for the soldier

Know the job: The primary concern of most soldiers is the leader's competence –"does he/she know what he/she is doing?" It is the responsibility of the leader to know the tasks required of his/her level of rank and experience as well as the tasks of his/her soldiers. When he/she can demonstrate such competence in combat, he/she gains the confidence and respect of his/her soldiers. You cannot evaluate your soldier's job unless you know it.

Know your soldiers: As the leader gets to know the soldiers, he/she determines their reliability. He/she discovers those he/she can turn to in a crisis. He/she gives them responsibility wherever possible to develop them as potential leaders. The leader identifies those soldiers who may need to increase their competence and self-confidence through more intensive training. The leader also encourages those few soldiers who are marginal by pointing out that being an effective team member is important to their survival and to the survival of the unit in critical combat situations.

Develop your soldiers: Soldiers' job expectations will be strongly influenced by their need to survive. You must establish a phased program that gradually works your soldiers into their combat role without endangering their lives or the lives of those around them. Based on experience, the leader considers the time it takes to get used to the combat environment and gives soldiers time lines within which to develop. It is critical that the leader get feedback from soldiers with whom new members are placed, and also that he/she personally observes the soldiers' progress.

Structure the situation for your soldiers: The leader structures the situation by ensuring that soldiers are adequately informed. As time permits, the leader needs to tell them as much as he/she can about the "what" and "why" of his/her situation to counteract their fear and uncertainty of the unknown. The leader must make his/her presence known by moving among his/her soldiers, issuing verbal instruction, using arm and hand signals, using flares, or simply standing up and leading the soldiers when appropriate. Soldiers feel structure when they know that they all share the dangers and burdens equally. Dangerous jobs must be rotated among the soldiers, and it must be evident that the leader shares the dangers too. Finally, the leader can structure the situation by realistically minimizing the perceived threat. The leader and the soldiers must be constantly aware that suppressing fearful behavior during combat is critical because it can spread from soldier to soldier and paralyze an entire unit.

Mission Focused

Soldiers are primarily committed to mission accomplishment rather than to self-interest. Each soldier is trained to do certain tasks that, when combined with tasks of other soldiers, accomplish the objective of the commander. Soldiers want to know as much as possible about the enemy and the battlefield environment in order to anticipate the enemy, make decisions quickly, favorably exploit the terrain, and win the battle. Unit missions and goals need to be firmly established in the soldiers' minds so that they have no questions about what the unit is trying to accomplish.

Mission accomplishment is learning, practicing, and becoming proficient in their job. Soldiers want to know what their assignment is, what is expected of them, and what the standards are by which they can measure their accomplishment.

Knowledge of unit history is also important to the soldiers' membership in the unit. The more positive things they know about the unit, the easier it is for them to identify with it. To sustain soldiers in the crisis of combat, it helps to include examples of "when things went wrong." Such examples can emphasize how predecessors did not give up and showed remarkable endurance, flexibility, and, when necessary, self-sacrifice to gain the ultimate victory.

Teaching Soldiers Duty-Related Skills

Teaching imparts knowledge or skills to others, causing them to learn by example or experience. In order to develop your soldiers, you must be able to demonstrate the technical and tactical skills you expect them to perform; otherwise, they will not listen to you. Teaching is passing on knowledge and skills to your soldiers. It is the number one task for all leaders. Teaching focuses primarily on technical and tactical skills. To be an Army leader, you must be a teacher; you give your soldiers knowledge and skills all the time, whether in formal classroom settings or through your example.

To be an effective teacher, you must first be professionally competent; then you must create conditions in which your soldiers can learn. How well you teach will be the measuring stick of how well your soldiers learn. In most cases, your soldiers will learn more by performing a skill than they will by watching you do it. Soldiers learn:

- Through the example of others.
- By forming a picture in their minds of what they are trying to learn.
- By absorbing information.
- Through practice (hands-on experience).

Teaching is a complex art that you must learn in addition to the competencies that you seek to teach. There are techniques and methods involved in teaching that have nothing to do with how good you are on the job. (FM 25-101 addresses areas related to conducting training.)

Good leaders know how important training is, which is why they:

- Help soldiers cope with stress.
- Play a key role in individual soldier training.
- Gain confidence and respect from the soldiers.
- Give soldiers responsibility when possible.
- Increase soldiers' competence and self-confidence.
- Get feedback from the soldiers.
- Structure the situation.
- Rotate dangerous jobs among the soldiers.
- Ensure the unit goals are firmly understood by the soldiers.
- Have knowledge of unit history and pass it on to the soldiers.
- Demonstrate technical and tactical skills.
- Pass on knowledge and skills to the soldiers.
- Are professionally competent teachers.

Part Seven
Responsibility and Accountability

Today's leaders are responsible for developing each soldier's potential and to give competent soldiers authority and responsibility. NCOs are responsible for assisting and advising officers in carrying out their duties. Accomplishing the Army's mission demands that officers and NCOs work together and advise, assist, and learn from one another. Officers and NCOs must determine the best types of responsibilities and tasks of each based on individual abilities and personalities. When NCOs are responsible for a task, they are also liable, or accountable, for the outcome. Responsibilities fall into two categories: individual and command.

Soldiers have individual responsibilities. They are responsible for their own actions. Nobody gives or delegates individual accountability. Command responsibilities refer to collective or organizational accountability and include how well units perform their mission. For example, the platoon sergeant is responsible for all the tasks and missions assigned to his/her platoon, as directed by the platoon leader; at the same time the mess sergeant is responsible for all the cooks.

Care and Maintenance of Equipment/Facilities

Part III, block "c," is where the rater tells about your daily duties and scope, including your soldiers, equipment, facilities, and dollar values. The soldiers, equipment, and facilities that your rater speaks of in block "c," part III, of the NCO-ER (DA form 2166-8) are your responsibility. As a leader, you must know the equipment and how to operate it. Good leaders know how to operate their equipment and ensure their soldiers do the same; they set the example with a hand-on approach. When new equipment arrives, the leader is the first one to find out how it works and then train his/her soldiers to do the same. The place where your soldiers live and work is also your responsibility. You must ensure they maintain it and keep it in good shape.

Soldier and Equipment Safety

NCOs must train their soldiers, and the training must be effective, to sustain a combat-ready Army and reduce human-error accidents. Training to standards produces skilled, disciplined soldiers who accept responsibility for the safety of themselves and others and for the protection of Army equipment. All training should be accomplished without unnecessarily risking the safety of soldiers or equipment. Careless accidents can significantly harm unit cohesion and teamwork. The leader must be concerned enough for the soldiers' safety and survival in combat to provide tough and challenging training. The training needs to be hard, yet safe. Equipment safety is just as important as soldier safety. Each year, in the Army, a soldier is crushed between a truck and some other object or another truck, or another soldier gets his/her hand caught in a machine. Make safety important in your unit before a soldier is hurt or killed.

Conservation of Supplies and Funds

You as a leader must master the skills of conservation, which includes time, equipment, facilities, budgets, and the soldiers. You must aggressively manage the resources you have at your disposal to ensure the unit readiness. You must skillfully evaluate objectives, anticipate resource equipment, and efficiently allocate what is available. You must balance available resources with organizational requirements and distribute them in a way that best achieves organizational goals in combat as well as peacetime.

Encouraging Soldiers to Learn and Grow

As a leader, you must know and care for your soldiers. You need to understand what makes them "tick" and learn what is important to them in life. As you train and care for your soldiers, you must encourage them to care for themselves by setting goals and doing all they can to reach them. Send all your PFCs and E-4's to "The Soldier of the Month" board; this will help prepare them for the E-5 promotion board. Your challenge as a leader is to attain, sustain, and enforce high standards of combat readiness through tough, realistic training, designed to develop and challenge each soldier. When soldiers are learning new tasks, tell them what you want done and show them how to do it. Let them try, and watch their performance. Accept performance that meets your standards; reward performance that exceeds your standards; correct performance that does not meet your standards. Determine the cause of the poor performance and take appropriate action. Give your soldiers the confidence they need to trust you as their leader. Train and cross-train them until they have confidence in the team's technical and tactical abilities. Remember, you influence your soldiers by what you say, write, and, most of all, what you do. Encourage them to learn, and show them how to become a great NCO like yourself.

Responsible for Good, Bad, Right, and Wrong

Most NCOs will stand out front when something good happens and take responsibility for it. A good NCO will stand out front when something good, bad, right, or wrong happens. You are responsible for training your soldiers to do their jobs and for understudying your leader in the event you must assume those duties. You must avoid evading responsibility by placing the blame on someone else. Seek responsibility and take responsibility for your and your soldiers' actions. Develop a sense of responsibility in your soldiers as you lead them into becoming the leaders of tomorrow. Each time you get promoted in the Army you get more responsibility, which means you are accountable for more also. Remember, to be or become a good leader you must be accountable and responsible for what you are in charge of and sometimes more. You must:

- Develop your soldiers' potential.
- Give competent soldiers authority and responsibility.
- Assist and advise officers and other NCOs.
- Determine responsibilities for individual soldiers' abilities.
- Be accountable for the outcome of your own actions.
- Be responsible for all your section equipment.
- Be the first to operate new equipment.
- Have effective training.
- Train without taking unnecessary risks.
- Provide tough and challenging training.
- Master the skills of conservation.
- Aggressively manage your resources.
- Understand what makes your soldiers "tick."
- Learn what is important to your soldiers.
- Encourage your soldiers to care for themselves.
- Set reachable goals for yourself and your soldiers.
- Enforce high standards through realistic training.
- Determine the cause for poor performance.
- Encourage your soldiers to learn and grow.
- Be responsible for the good, bad, right, and wrong.
- Develop a sense of responsibility for your soldier.

PART EIGHT
Overall Performance and Potential

There are only five blocks for rating in Part V, and two of them are for the rater. Many raters and senior raters think Part V is just for the senior rater, which is not true. However, many senior raters will go along with the rater rating and align their rating with his/hers. At the same time, some senior raters may not feel the rater is doing a good job in rating the rated NCO and, for that reason, will rate the rated NCO better than the rater did.

The senior rater box markings are independent of the rater box markings. There are no specific box marking requirements of the senior rater that are based on the rater box markings. Part V is structured for the NCO potential for overall performance and potential. It consists of and includes the rater box markings for promotion and service potential; the rater's specific position recommendation; the senior rater's overall performance and potential; and the senior rater's choice of alternative for future performance.

When the senior rater does not meet the minimum time requirement for evaluating the rated NCO, the statement "Does not meet minimum qualifications" will be placed in block (e) of Part V of the NCO-ER. The senior rater's bullet comments should focus on potential, but may address performance and/or evaluation rendered by the rater. He/she must also comment on marginal, fair, or poor rating in Part V. The rater has only two blocks for rating the rated NCO in Part V. The first block (a) is the rated NCO's overall potential for promotion and/or service in position of greater responsibility.

The Rater's Overall Performance and Potential Ratings

Overall performance and potential consist of, and include, the rater box marking for promotion/service potential; rater specific positions recommendation; and the senior rater bullet comments; overall performance and overall potential for promotion and/or service in position of greater responsibility. The rater part for overall performance and potential is found in Part V (a) and (b). Part V (a) is for overall potential for promotion and/or service in position of greater responsibility. As you can see, Part V (a) can be rated in three areas, which are:

- Overall potential for promotion
- Overall potential for service in positions of greater responsibility

- Overall potential for promotion and service in positions of greater responsibility

There are no bullet comments for the rater in Part V (a); however, the rater should place an "X" in one of the three boxes, which are:

- **Among the Best**: This means the NCO has demonstrated a very good solid performance and is a strong recommendation for promotion and/or service in a position of greater responsibility.
- **Fully Capable**: The NCO has demonstrated a good performance and is a strong recommendation for promotion should sufficient allocation be available.
- **Marginal**: The NCO has demonstrated poor performance and should not be promoted at this time.

In block V (a) the rater will place an "X" in the "Among the Best," "Fully Capable," or "Marginal" box. His/her rating should be made after reviewing his/her rating in the "Excellence," "Success," or "Need improvement" ratings, in blocks (b), (c), (d), (e), and (f), and in addition, the "YES" or "NO" blocks in Part IV (a), numbers 1-7.

Among the Best

Let's take a closer look at this rating. The NCO who gets this rating is one who may have one or two "Excellence" ratings in Part IV (b), (c), (d), (e), and (f) and all "YES" ratings in part IV (a). If the NCO does not get one or two "Excellence" ratings in Part IV (b-f), he/she should get all "Success" ratings in blocks (b-f) of Part IV along with two or three bullet comments in Part IV (b-f). Three bullet comments in these blocks help justify the "Among the Best" rating. The "Among the Best" rating is the best rating an NCO can receive on his/her NCO-ER because even if an NCO gets all "Excellence" ratings in IV (b-f), he/she would still receive the "Among the Best" rating. Remember, the Army goal is that all NCOs get "Success" ratings in blocks (b-f) of Part IV.

The "Among the Best" rating also means that the NCO has a very strong recommendation for promotion and/or service in a position of greater responsibility. This is the best rating to get a NCO promoted because – for example, you have an E-5 whom you want promoted to E-6 – you can put a bullet comment in Part IV (d) that reads:

- promote now
- should be promoted soon
- should make next cut-off
- promoted ahead of peers
- promotion will justify his/her duty performance

After you write a good bullet comment in Part IV (d), you can then place a comment in Part V (b) that reads:

- make him/her section chief
- will make a good team leader
- ready to take over section

Fully Capable

The "Fully Capable" NCO demonstrates a good performance, whereas the "Among the Best" NCO demonstrates a very good, solid performance. You can get a "Success" rating in Part IV (b), (c), (d), (e), and (f) and get the "Fully Capable" rating. This is what is called a "center line" NCO-ER.

"Center line" is what most NCOs receive on their NCO-ER. Remember, you can get all "Success" ratings in IV (b-f) and also the "Among the Best" rating in Part V (a), but you must have two or three very strong bullet comments in Part IV (b-f) and all "YES" box markings in Part IV (a).

The "Fully Capable" NCO also has a strong recommendation for promotion but only if sufficient allocation is available. "Sufficient" means enough to meet the needs of a situation, so if there are not enough stripes left over from the "Among the Best" NCOs in your MOS you may not get promoted if your NCO-ER is not better than the other NCOs in your MOS. Remember, more NCOs will get promoted from the "Fully Capable" rating because there are more NCOs in the "Fully Capable" rating zone than there are in the "Among the Best" rating zone.

Marginal

You must make sure you never get a "Marginal" rating on your NCO-ER. A "Marginal" rating means you had demonstrated poor job performance. Poor performance is less than adequate performance. Again, you never want to get a "Marginal" rating in Part V (a) of your NCO-ER, because you will have to live with it for up to five years.

You see, when your NCO-ER is looked at for promotion, assignment, or retention in the Army at DA, your last five reports are what will be viewed. Should you get a "Marginal" report during this rating period and your report is being looked at for promotion, assignment, or retention, the evaluators will not only look at your present report, but also the last four reports before the now "Marginal" report. They will look at the last four to see how your duty performance was doing up to this point, and also try to see or get an idea as to what may have caused you to get the "Marginal" report. If your last four reports were "Fully Capable" reports, they will look very closely at your rater and senior rater comments and Part V (b-e). As for being promoted with a "Marginal" report, forget it. A "Marginal" report means you should not get promoted at this time, and it could very well stop you from getting promoted during the next four reports unless you go from the "Marginal" rating to the "Among the Best" rating. To evaluate your overall performance and potential, ask yourself:

- Have I demonstrated very good job performance?
- Can I serve well in the next duty position?
- Can I handle more responsibility?
- Do I have a good recommendation for promotion?
- Will I get an "Excellence" or "Success" rating?
- Will I get strong bullet comments on my NCO-ER?
- How do I compare with my peers on my NCO-ER?
- Are Parts IV and V on my NCO-ER "center line"?
- Is my NCO-ER "Among the Best" in my MOS?
- Do I keep away from the "Marginal" reports?

The next rater's block in Part V is block (b). Here the rater can list three positions in which the rated NCO could best serve the Army at his/her current or next higher grade. At least two duty positions should be entered but no more than three (three is better). Should the NCO be rated "Among the Best," block (b) should show two or three areas he/she could best serve the Army in his/her next grade because an "Among the Best" rating means the rated NCO should be promoted. At the same time, if the NCO receives a "Marginal" rating, the two or three positions in which he/she could best serve the Army may show the one he/she is now serving plus one or two below the position he/she is now holding.

Part Nine
Senior Rater Overall Performance and Potential Rating

The first senior rater block is block (c), in which the senior rater will rate the rated NCO on his/her overall performance. In order to do that, he/she can rate the rated NCO as "Successful" with a number 1, 2, or 3, or he/she could rate the rated NCO "Fair" or "Poor." If the senior rater rates the rated NCO "Successful" with a number 1, it means that the NCO has a very good job performance and is a strong recommendation for promotion. This rating is about the same as the "Among the Best" rating. If the senior rater rates the rated NCO "Successful" with a number 2, it means the rating is about the same as the number 1 rating but not as strong. A "Successful" rating with a 3 means the rated NCO has a good performance and should be promoted if sufficient promotion allocations are available. As you can see, this rating is about the same as the rater's "Fully Capable" rating.

A "Fair" rating by the senior rater means the rated NCO may require additional training/observation and should not be promoted at this time-which is the same as the rater's "Marginal" rating. The worst rating an NCO can receive from the senior rater-and one that can cause him/her to be put out of the Army – is the "Poor" rating. A "Poor" rating means that the NCO is weak or deficient and, in the opinion of the senior rater, needs significant improvement or training in one or more areas. It also means "do not promote."

The next block for the senior rater is block (d), which is for the rated NCO's overall potential for promotion and/or service in a position of greater responsibility. The rating in this block has the same meaning as block (c), except that the senior rater will rate the rated NCO "Superior" with the numbers 1, 2, or 3 instead of "Successful" with the numbers 1, 2, or 3.

Part Ten
Senior Rater's Bullet Comments

The next and last block is block (e), which is for the senior rater's bullet comments. In this block, he/she can write up to five bullet comments. The rules for the senior rater's bullet comments are as follows:

- Bullet comments are mandatory for the "Excellence" or "Needs Improvement" ratings.
- The senior rater must address the "Marginal" rating in Part V (a) and the "Fair" or "Poor" rating in Part V (c and d).
- Bullet comments should focus on potential, but may address performance and/or the evaluation rendered by the rater. If the senior rater meets the minimum time requirement for evaluation, he/she must make bullet comments.

4

Why Bullet Comments Are Important

So far, we have looked over what the Army expects you to do as an NCO. What is more important is that you know now what you need to do so the evaluators at DA know you are the leader the Army wants you to be. We went over the ten ratable parts of the NCO-ER, which give you an idea as to what you need to do in order to get that "Successful" or "Excellence" rating; however, I cannot begin to tell you how important it is to get bullet comments for ratable parts of the NCO-ER. Before I get into a discussion of the bullet comments, let us take a close look at what the NCO-ER was designed to do, why the counseling checklist/record is important, the rules for bullet comments, and prohibited comments.

What the NCO-ER Was Designed to Do

The non-commissioned officer evaluation reporting system is designed to:

- Strengthen the ability of the NCO corps to meet the professional challenges of the future through the indoctrination of Army values and basic NCO responsibilities.

- Ensure the selection of the best qualified non-commissioned officers to serve in positions of increasing responsibility by providing the rating chain view of performance/potential for use in centralized selection, assignment, and other enlisted personnel management system decisions.

- Contribute to Army-wide improved performance and professional development by increased emphasis on performance counseling.

- Ensure sound personnel management decisions can be made and that an NCO's potential can be fully developed.

Why the Counseling Checklist/Record Is Important

The purpose of the counseling checklist is to improve performance counseling by providing structure and discipline as well as improving performance. The rater will use DA form 2166-8-1, along with a working copy of the NCO-ER (2166-8), to prepare for, conduct, and record results of performance counseling with the rated NCO. The process for the rated NCO counseling is as follows:

1. During the first counseling session with the rated NCO, the rater should specifically let the rated NCO know what is expected during the rating period. He/she should show the rated NCO the rating chain and a complete duty description, discuss the meaning of the values and responsibilities contained on the NCO-ER, and explain the standards for success. Before the rated NCO leaves the counseling session, the rater records key points discussed and obtains the rated NCO's initials on page 2 of DA form 2166-8-1.

2. The rater will conduct later counseling sessions during the rating period; they will be conducted at least quarterly. These coun-

seling sessions differ from the first counseling session in that the primary focus is on observed action and demonstrated behavior and results, discussing what was done well and what could be done better. The goal of performance counseling is to get all NCOs to be successful and meet or exceed standards. Before the NCO leaves the counseling session, the rater should:

- Record counseling dates on DA form 2166-8-1, which are to be placed in Part III (f) of DA form 2166-8.
- Write any additional key points that came up during the counseling session on DA form 2166-8.
- Show key points to the rated NCO and get his/her initials.
- Save the NCO-ER with the checklist for the next counseling session.

Rules for Bullet Comments

Bullet comments will:

- Be short, concise, to the point. They will not be longer than two lines, preferably one, and no more than one bullet comment to a line.

- Start with action words (verbs) or possessive pronouns (his/her). Do not use the NCO's name or the personal pronouns he/she. Should use the "past" tense when addressing the NCO's performance and/or contributions.

- Be double-spaced between bullets.

- Be preceded by a small "o" to designate the start of the comment.

- Each comment should start with a small letter unless the initial word is a proper noun.

Before completing the evaluation portion of Part IV, the following must be considered:

- Values/NCO Responsibilities
- Commander's evaluation (CE)
- Common task test (CTT)
- Army Physical Fitness Test (APFT)
- Weapon qualifications
- Army weight control program (AR600-9)
- Values, Part IV (a) – The rater will check either a "YES" or "NO" in the Values block. Mandatory specific bullet comments are required for all "NO" entries. Each entry should be based on whether the rated NCO "meets" or "does not meet" the standard for each particular value. Bullet comments are used to explain any area where the rated NCO is particularly strong or needs improvement.
- The rater explains, with specific bullet examples, any area where the rated NCO demonstrated excellence, notable success, or needs improvement. Specific bullet examples are mandatory for an "Excellence" or "Needs Improvement" rating. A specific bullet example can be used only once; therefore, the rater must decide under which responsibility the bullet fits best.

Part IV (c), Army Physical Fitness Test bullet comments are mandatory for the following reason:

- The rater will explain an APFT entry of "FAIL" or "PROFILE." Comments on "FAIL" entries will address reasons for failure and note any progress toward meeting physical fitness standards. Comments on "PROFILE" (permanent or temporary) will describe the rated NCO's ability to perform assigned duties. Note, however, that if an NCO has appeared before an MOS medical retention board and been determined fit for duty and deployable, rating officials may not state that the profile hinders duty performance.

- An APFT entry is not required for pregnant NCOs, who are exempt from the APFT IAW AR 40-501. For pregnant NCOs who have not taken the APFT within the last 12 months due to pregnancy convalescent leave and temporary profile, the rater will enter the following statement in Part IV (c): "Exempt from APFT requirement IAW AR 40-501."

Part IV (c), Height and Weight comments:

Rater's specific bullet examples are mandatory in Part IV (c) for the following:

- To explain the absence of the height and weight data.

- To explain any entry of "NO," indicating noncompliance with the standards of AR 600-9. These comments will indicate the reason for noncompliance. Medical conditions may be cited for noncompliance; however, the "NO" entry is still required because medical waivers to weight control standards are not permitted for evaluation report purpose. The process or lack of progress in a weight control program will be indicated.

- The entire entry is left blank for pregnant NCOs. The rater will enter the following bullet in Part IV (c): "Exempt from weight control standards IAW AR 600-9."

Prohibited Comments

- The use of inappropriate or arbitrary remarks or comments that draw attention to difference relating to race, color, religion, gender, age, or national origin is prohibited.

- No mention will be made of any punitive or administrative action taken (or planned) against a rated NCO.

- No evaluation comments, favorable or unfavorable, will be based solely on an NCO's marital status.

- Evaluation comments will not be made about the employment, education, or volunteer activities of an NCO's spouse.

- An NCO who voluntarily enters the (ADAPCP) should not be penalized by mentioning it on his/her NCO-ER.

- Rating officials cannot use information derived from (ADAPCP) records in their evaluation.

- An NCO's voluntary entry into (ADAPCP) or successful rehabilitation should be mentioned as a factor to the rated NCO's credit.

- Each report will be an independent evaluation of the rated NCO for a specific rating period. It will not refer to prior or subsequent reports.

Bullet Comments

A bullet comment is a statement that may or may not have a verb, object, or subject. It is a short, concise comment used by raters to justify their evaluation. Your rater and senior rater do not have to write a bullet comment for you unless you get a "NO" entry in Part IV (a) or an "Excellence" or "Needs Improvement" rating in Part IV (b-f). The rater does not have to write a bullet comment for the "Success" rating; however, if you get a "Success" rating in leadership or another area with no bullet comment and one of your peers gets the same rating with a bullet comment, who do you think DA will feel is the better NCO? Another thing you need to check out is the rater rating in Part V (a) and the senior rater rating in Part V (c) and (d). The ratings must align with each other as follows:

RATER	SENIOR RATER
Among the Best	Successful, with a number 1
Among the Best	Successful, with a number 2
Fully Capable	Successful with a number 3
Marginal	Fair
Needs Improvement	Poor

5

Questions All Leaders
Should Be Able to Answer

QUESTION: What is leadership style?

ANSWER: Leadership style is the personal manner and approach of leading, providing purpose, direction, and motivation. It is the way leaders directly interact with their soldiers.

QUESTION: How many basic styles of military leadership are there?

ANSWER: There are three basic styles of military leadership.

QUESTION: What are the three basic styles of leadership?

ANSWER: The three basic styles of leadership are directing, participating, and delegating.

QUESTION: Explain the directing style of military leadership.

ANSWER: The directing style of military leadership is when the leader tells the soldiers what, how, when, and where he/she wants something done, and he/she closely supervises them to ensure directions are followed.

QUESTION: Explain the participating style of leadership.
ANSWER: The participating style of military leadership is when the leader involves soldiers in determining what to do and how to do it.

QUESTION: Explain the delegating style of military leadership.
ANSWER: The delegating style of leadership is where the leader delegates a problem-solving and decision-making authority to a soldier or to a group of soldiers.

QUESTION: Which leadership style is best?
ANSWER: The best leadership style is the one that meets the situation and the needs of the soldiers.

QUESTION: What must you understand when choosing a style of leadership?
ANSWER: When choosing a style of leadership you must understand the four major factors of leadership, which are:
- Those who are being led
- The leader
- The situation
- Communication

QUESTION: Which leadership style is most efficient?
ANSWER: The most efficient style of leadership is the delegating style.

QUESTION: Why is the delegating style the most efficient?
ANSWER: The delegating style is the most efficient because it requires the least amount of your time and energy to interact, direct, and communicate with your soldiers.

QUESTION: What must you do before using the delegating style of leadership?

ANSWER: Before using the delegating style of leadership, you must train and develop your soldiers.

QUESTION: When should you be flexible in your leadership style?

ANSWER: You should be flexible in your leadership style as the mission changes or as new tasks are assigned.

QUESTION: What type of leaders would soldiers prefer to be led by?

ANSWER: Soldiers prefer to be led by leaders who provide strength, inspiration, and guidance, and will help them become winners.

QUESTION: What must you BE as a leader?

ANSWER: As a leader, you must BE:
- a person of strong and honorable character
- committed to the professional Army ethic
- an example of individual values
- able to resolve complex ethical dilemmas.

QUESTION: What must you KNOW as a leader?

ANSWER: As a leader, you must KNOW:
- The four major factors of leadership and how they affect each other
- Standards, yourself, human nature, your job, and your unit

QUESTION: What must you DO as a leader?

ANSWER: As a leader, what you must DO is provide purpose, direction, and motivation.

QUESTION: How should effective leaders deal with soldiers?

ANSWER: Effective leaders should deal with soldiers differently, as a situation or mission changes.

QUESTION: What kind of leaders will future wars be won by?

ANSWER: Future wars will be won by leaders with strong and honorable character.

QUESTION: What are the three pillars for developing leaders?

ANSWER: The three pillars for developing leaders are Institutional Training, Operational Assignment, and Self Development.

QUESTION: What do the three pillars for developing leaders provide?

ANSWER: The three pillars for developing leaders provide education, training, and experience needed to develop Skills, Knowledge, and Attitudes (SKA).

QUESTION: What reference governs Army military leadership?

ANSWER: The reference that governs Army military leadership is FM 22-100.

QUESTION: What are the two purposes of FM 22-100?

ANSWER: The two purposes of FM 22-100 are to provide an overview of Army leadership and prescribe the necessary leadership to be effective in peace or war.

QUESTION: Who are the primary leaders that FM 22-100 focuses on?

ANSWER: The primary leaders that FM 22-100 focuses on are company grade officers, warrant officers, NCOs, and junior leaders at battalion level, squadron level, and below.

QUESTION: What seven fundamental expectations does FM 22-100 address?

ANSWER: The seven fundamental expectations that FM 22-100 addresses are:

- Demonstrate tactical and technical competence
- Teach soldiers
- Be a good listener
- Treat soldiers with dignity and respect
- Stress the basics
- Set the example
- Set and enforce standards

QUESTION: What is the fundamental mission of the Army?

ANSWER: The fundamental mission of the Army is to deter war and win in combat.

QUESTION: What type of soldiers can accomplish any mission?

ANSWER: The well led, properly trained, highly motivated and inspired soldiers can accomplish any mission.

QUESTION: What type of leader is the Army looking for?

ANSWER: The Army is looking for leaders who:
- Understand the human dimension of operations
- provide purpose, direction, and motivation to their units
- show initiative
- are willing to exploit opportunities and take well calculated risks within the commander's intent
- build cohesive teams
- communicate effectively, both orally and in writing
- are committed to the professional Army ethic

QUESTION: How can a respected leader influence soldiers?

ANSWER: A respected leader can influence soldiers by teaching, coaching, counseling, training, disciplining, and setting the example.

QUESTION: What are the four types of communication skills NCOs should possess to become effective leaders?

ANSWER: The four types of communication skills NCOs should possess to become effective leaders are reading, writing, speaking, and listening.

QUESTION: What must you BE-KNOW-DO as a leader?
ANSWER: As a leader you must:
- BE a person of strong and honorable character; committed to the professional Army ethic; and serve as an example of the individual values that will enable you to resolve complex ethical dilemmas.
- KNOW the four factors of leadership and how they affect each other: you must know standards, yourself, human nature, and your job.
- DO provide purpose, direction, and motivation.

QUESTION: As leaders, what must we do better than the enemy to succeed in war?
ANSWER: To succeed in a war as leaders, we must have better prepared leaders, soldiers, and units.

QUESTION: As a leader, what challenges will you face?
ANSWER: As a leader, you will face the challenges of taking care of your soldiers' needs; developing them into cohesive teams; training them under tough, realistic conditions to demanding standards; assess their personal and professional growth; and reward them for their successes.

QUESTION: What must a leader do in order to meet the challenge?
ANSWER: To meet the challenge, the leader must be competent, and confident in their ability to lead.

QUESTION: What are the nine leadership competencies?
ANSWER: The nine leadership competencies are:
1. Communication
2. Supervision

3. Teaching and Counseling
4. Soldier Team Development
5. Technical and Tactical Proficiency
6. Decision-Making
7. Planning
8. Use of Available Systems
9. Professional Ethics

QUESTION: What do the nine leadership competencies provide?
ANSWER: The nine leadership competencies provide a framework for leadership development and assessment, and establish broad categories of skills, knowledge, and attitudes (SKA) that define leadership behavior.

QUESTION: When and how were the nine leadership competencies developed?
ANSWER: The nine leadership competencies were developed in 1976. The study was conducted by a group of leaders ranking from corporal to general officers.

QUESTION: What should the leaders ask about themselves?
ANSWER: Leader should ask themselves who they are, who do they think they are, and what do others think of them.

QUESTION: What must an effective leader clearly understand?
ANSWER: An effective leader must clearly understand discipline and cohesion.

QUESTION: What does providing a PURPOSE do for the soldier?
ANSWER: Providing a PURPOSE gives the soldier a reason why he/she should participate in dangerous activities under stressful circumstances.

QUESTION: What does providing DIRECTION give to the soldier?

ANSWER: Providing DIRECTION gives the soldier an orientation of tasks to be accomplished based on the priorities set by the leader.

QUESTION: What does providing MOTIVATION give to the soldier?
ANSWER: Providing MOTIVATION gives the soldier the will to do everything he/she is capable of doing to accomplish a mission.

QUESTION: How can leaders provide DIRECTION?
ANSWER: Leaders can provide DIRECTION by:
- Planning, training, and setting goals
- knowing and maintaining standards
- making decisions and solving problems
- supervising and evaluating
- coaching and counseling

QUESTION: What are the two responsibilities concerning standards that the leader must know?
ANSWER: The two responsibilities concerning standards that the leader must know are: what the standards are, and enforce established standards.

QUESTION: If the soldiers cannot meet the standards, what should the leader do?
ANSWER: If the soldiers cannot meet the standards, the leader should ask himself/herself:
- Did they understand what was expected?
- Did I provide the resources, authority, training, and direction needed?
- Did they know how to carry out the mission that was expected?
- Were they motivated to do what was expected?

QUESTION: What must leaders do in the midst of a FAST-PACED BATTLEFIELD?

ANSWER: In the midst of a FAST-PACED BATTLEFIELD, leaders must take initiative, make rapid decisions, motivate their soldiers, maneuver their units, apply firepower, and protect and sustain their forces.

QUESTION: What are some of the ways the Army establishes standards?

ANSWER: Some of the ways the Army establishes standards are through AR's laws, ARTEP, Mission Training Plans, Soldier Training Publications, Field and Training Manuals, General Defense Plans, and SOPs.

QUESTION: What is a disciplined soldier?

ANSWER: A disciplined soldier is one who is orderly, obedient, controlled, and dependable.

QUESTION: What are the nine principles of war recognized by the Army?

ANSWER: The nine principles of war recognized by the Army are:
1. Objective
2. Offensive
3. Mass
4. Economy of Force
5. Maneuver
6. Unity of Command
7. Security
8. Surprises
9. Simplicity

QUESTION: When is communicating to the soldier effective?

ANSWER: Communicating to the soldier is effective when he/she listens and understands your intent.

QUESTION: What is the ultimate goal of the Army?

ANSWER: The ultimate goal of the Army is to ensure that every soldier and unit are properly trained, motivated, and prepared to win in the event of a war.

QUESTION: What key points should you remember when developing goals?

ANSWER: The key points you should remember when developing goals are:
- Goals should be realistic and attainable.
- Goals should lead to improved combat readiness.
- Soldiers should be involved in the goal-setting process.
- You must develop a program to achieve each goal.

QUESTION: What should you remember when solving a problem?

ANSWER: When solving a problem, you should remember that a good decision made in time to implement it is better than the best decision made too late.

QUESTION: What are the steps in backward planning?

ANSWER: The steps in backward planning are:
- Determine the basics: what, how, and when.
- Identify tasks you want to accomplish and establish a sequence for them.
- Develop a schedule to accomplish the tasks you have identified, beginning with the last task to be accomplished and working back to the present time.

QUESTION: What are the five steps in the problem-solving process?

ANSWER: The five steps in the problem-solving process are:
1. Recognize and define the problem
2. Gather the facts and make assumptions
3. Develop possible solutions
4. Analyze and compare the possible solutions
5. Select the best solution

QUESTION: What is supervising?
ANSWER: Supervising is keeping a grasp on the situation and ensuring that plans and policies are implemented properly.

QUESTION: What is supervision?
ANSWER: Supervision is giving instructions and continuously inspecting the accomplishment of the task.

QUESTION: What are the downfalls of under-supervision?
ANSWER: The downfalls of under-supervision are that it can lead to frustration, miscommunication, and lack of coordination, disorganization, and having the perception that you do not care, which in turn can lead to resentment, low morale, and poor motivation.

QUESTION: How should you evaluate a soldier?
ANSWER: You should evaluate a soldier by looking at the way he/she accomplishes a task, checking first-hand and inspecting.

QUESTION: How do soldiers learn?
ANSWER: Soldiers learn by:
- Forming a picture in their minds of what they are trying to learn
- The example of others
- Gaining and understanding necessary information
- Application or practice

QUESTION: How do you convince your soldiers that they need to learn the tasks you are trying to teach them?
ANSWER: You convince your soldiers that they need to learn the tasks you are trying to teach them by showing them that mastery will make them more competent soldiers, enable them to do their duties and survive on the battlefield.

QUESTION: What is motivation?
ANSWER: Motivation is the cause of, or reason for, action.

QUESTION: What is stress?
ANSWER: Stress is the body's response to a demand placed on it.

QUESTION: How can you motivate your soldiers?
ANSWER: You can motivate your soldiers by:
- Serving as the ethical standard bearer
- Developing cohesive soldier teams
- Rewarding and punishing

QUESTION: Can stress be positive and enhance performance?
ANSWER: Yes, stress can be positive and enhance performance at low levels.

QUESTION: What is battle fatigue?
ANSWER: Battle fatigue is a term used to describe soldiers' negative reactions to the extreme stress on the battlefield.

QUESTION: What are some of the indications of battle fatigue?
ANSWER: Some of the indications of battle fatigue are: tension, aches, pains, dry mouth and pale skin, upset stomach, diarrhea, exhaustion, complaining, and insomnia.

QUESTION: What are some of the ways you can protect your soldiers and yourself from battle fatigue?
ANSWER: Some of the ways you can protect your soldiers and yourself from battle fatigue are:
- Ensure that your soldiers know what they are capable of doing.
- Have tough, demanding, and realistic training.
- Keep your soldiers informed about the situations.
- Do not let your soldiers exaggerate the enemy's capabilities.

- Do not let your soldiers exaggerate the difficulty of upcoming missions.
- Help soldiers talk through their problem.
- Develop and enforce a sleeping plan for the soldiers and yourself.

QUESTION: How can you treat battle-fatigued soldiers?

ANSWER: If possible and safe, you can treat battle-fatigued soldiers by ensuring that they:
- Sleep, and drink plenty of fluids
- Continue to eat normal portions of food
- Continue to conduct training
- Take time to attend to personal hygiene needs
- Talk about what happened (lessons learned)
- Share grief, talk out personal worries, and talk with the chaplain
- Keep busy when not resting
- See the medic

QUESTION: What are the six actions that a leader must take?

ANSWER: The six actions a leader must take are:
1. Lead the unit
2. Build cohesion
3. Develop confidence
4. Train the unit
5. Develop a physically fit unit
6. Develop a winning attitude

QUESTION: What is authority?

ANSWER: Authority is the legitimate power that leaders have, to direct soldiers or to take action within the scope of their responsibility.

QUESTION: Where does legal authority begin?

ANSWER: Legal authority begins with the Constitution.

QUESTION: How is Military Authority divided?
ANSWER: Military Authority is divided between Congress and the President.

QUESTION: What authority does Congress have over the Army?
ANSWER: Congress has the authority to make laws, which govern the Army.

QUESTION: What authority does the President have over the Army?
ANSWER: The President has the authority to command the Army as the Commander-in-Chief.

QUESTION: What is Commander Authority?
ANSWER: Commander Authority is the authority whose position requires the direction and control of other members in the Army.

QUESTION: What is General Military Authority?
ANSWER: General Military Authority is the authority extended to all soldiers to take action; it is originated in the oaths of officers, laws, rank structures, traditions, Uniform Code of Military Justice (UCMJ), and regulations.

QUESTION: What authority does a leader have over soldiers from another unit?
ANSWER: The leader has General Military Authority over soldiers from another unit.

QUESTION: What are the two categories of responsibilities?
ANSWER: The two categories of responsibilities are individual and command.

QUESTION: Who has individual responsibilities?
ANSWER: All soldiers have individual responsibilities and assumed them when they took their oath of enlistment.

QUESTION: What do command responsibilities refer to?

ANSWER: Command responsibilities refer to collective or organizational accountability and include how well units perform their mission.

QUESTION: How many chains of command does the Army have?

ANSWER: The Army has one chain of command, which is the officers' chain of command.

QUESTION: What is the NCO support channel?

ANSWER: The NCO support channel is the NCO chain that parallels and reinforces the chain of command.

QUESTION: What do the chain of command and the NCO support channel have in common?

ANSWER: Both the chain of command and the NCO support channel are a means of control and communication.

QUESTION: The battalion or higher-level NCO support channel begins with whom?

ANSWER: The battalion or higher-level NCO support channel begins with the command sergeant major and ends with section chiefs, squad leaders, or team leaders.

QUESTION: What is the purpose of leadership development?

ANSWER: The purpose of leadership development is to develop leaders who will be capable of maintaining a trained and ready Army in peacetime to deter war.

QUESTION: List the five manuals containing the Army's leadership doctrine.

ANSWER: The five manuals containing the Army's leadership doctrine are:
1. FM 22-100 Military Leadership
2. FM 22-101 Leadership Counseling

3. FM 22-102 Soldier Team Development
4. FM 22-103 Leadership and Command at Senior Levels
5. FM 25-100 Training the Force

QUESTION: What does FM 22-100 specify for the leaders?
ANSWER: FM 22-100 specifies a direct face-to-face mode to the leaders.

QUESTION: What does FM 22-101 specify for the leaders?
ANSWER: FM 22-101 specifies conduct and leadership counseling to the leaders.

QUESTION: What does FM 22-102 specify for the leaders?
ANSWER: FM 22-102 specifies the development of soldier teams at company level and below that can meet the challenges of combat to the leaders.

QUESTION: What does FM 22-103 specify for the leaders?
ANSWER: FM 22-103 specifies the principles and framework for leading and commanding at senior levels.

QUESTION: What does FM 25-100 provide for the leaders?
ANSWER: FM 25-100 provides expectations and standards on training doctrines for the leaders.

QUESTION: Is it the intent of FM 22-100 to tell leaders exactly how to lead?
ANSWER: No, leaders must be themselves and apply the leadership doctrine in the situations they will face as leaders.

QUESTION: What are norms?
ANSWER: Norms are the rules or laws normally based on agreed-upon beliefs and values that members of a group follow to live in harmony.

QUESTION: What are the two categories of norms?

ANSWER: The two categories of norms are formal and informal.

QUESTION: Why are beliefs, values, and norms important?

ANSWER: Beliefs, values, and norms are important because they guide the actions of individuals and the group by giving direction, meaning, and purpose to their lives.

QUESTION: What are beliefs?

ANSWER: Beliefs are assumptions or convictions a person holds as true about something, a concept, or another person.

QUESTION: What are values?

ANSWER: Values are attitudes about the worth or importance of people and concepts.

QUESTION: What are the seven Individual Values that all soldiers are expected to possess?

ANSWER: The seven Individual Values that all soldiers are expected to possess are:
1. Loyalty
2. Duty
3. Respect
4. Selfless-service
5. Honor
6. Integrity
7. Personal courage

QUESTION: What is Loyalty?

ANSWER: Loyalty is to bear true faith and allegiance to the U.S. Constitution, the Army, your unit, and other soldiers.

QUESTION: What is Duty?
ANSWER: Duty begins with everything required of you by law; it is no more than "fulfill your obligations."

QUESTION: What is Respect?
ANSWER: Respect means recognizing and appreciating the inherent dignity and worth of all people, and treating people as they should be treated.

QUESTION: What is Selfless-service?
ANSWER: Selfless-service is putting the welfare of the nation, Army, and soldiers before your own; it means doing what is right for the nation, Army, your organization, and your soldiers, and putting these responsibilities above your own interest.

QUESTION: What is Honor?
ANSWER: Honor holds Army values together while at the same time being a value itself; it means living up to all the Army values.

QUESTION: What is Integrity?
ANSWER: Integrity means doing what is legally and morally right.

QUESTION: What is Personal courage?
ANSWER: Personal courage is facing fear, danger, or adversity; it is the ability to put fear aside and do what is necessary.

QUESTION: What four leadership requirements must the leader satisfy?
ANSWER: The four leadership requirements the leader must satisfy are:
1. Lead in peace to be prepared for war
2. Develop individual leaders

3. Develop leadership teams
4. Decentralize

QUESTION: What are the eleven principles of leadership?
ANSWER: The eleven principles of leadership are:
1. Know yourself and seek self-improvement.
2. Be technically and tactically proficient.
3. Seek responsibility and take responsibility for your actions.
4. Make sound and timely decisions.
5. Set the example.
6. Know your soldiers and look out for their well-being.
7. Keep your soldiers informed.
8. Develop a sense of responsibility in your soldiers.
9. Ensure the task is understood, supervised, and accomplished.
10. Build the team.
11. Employ your unit in accordance with its capabilities.

QUESTION: When were the principles of leadership developed?
ANSWER: The principles of leadership were developed in 1948 during a leadership study.

QUESTION: When were the principles of leadership first included in leadership doctrine?
ANSWER: The principles of leadership were first included in leadership doctrine in 1951.

QUESTION: What is physical courage?
ANSWER: Physical courage is overcoming fears of bodily harm and doing your duty.

QUESTION: What is moral courage?
ANSWER: Moral courage is overcoming fears of other than fears of bodily harm while doing what needs to be done.

QUESTION: What is candor?
ANSWER: Candor is being frank, open, honest, and sincere with your soldiers, seniors, and peers; it is an expression of personal integrity.

QUESTION: What is competence?
ANSWER: Competence is proficiency in required professional knowledge, judgment, and skills.

QUESTION: What does commitment mean?
ANSWER: Commitment means the dedication to carry out all unit missions and to serve the values of the country, the Army, and the unit.

QUESTION: What impact can beliefs have on the leader?
ANSWER: The beliefs of the climate, cohesion, discipline, training, and combat effectiveness of a unit can have a direct impact on the leader.

QUESTION: What are the two modes of leadership?
ANSWER: The two modes of leadership are direct and indirect modes.

QUESTION: Schools, experience, and self-development are three equally important pillars for what?
ANSWER: Schools, experience, and self-development are three equally important pillars for developing individual leaders.

QUESTION: What is character?
ANSWER: Character is a person's inner strength and is the link between values and behaviors.

QUESTION: How can the leader influence beliefs, values, and norms?

ANSWER: The leader can influence beliefs, values, and norms by setting the example and recognizing behavior that supports professional beliefs, values, and norms; and by planning, executing, and assessing tough, realistic individual and collective training.

QUESTION: What is the meaning of "Soldier of Character"?
ANSWER: "Soldier of Character" is a term used to identify a soldier with strong and honorable character.

QUESTION: How can soldiers build strong and honorable character?
ANSWER: Soldiers can build strong and honorable character by hard work, study, and challenging experiences.

QUESTION: What are the four elements of Army ethics?
ANSWER: The four elements of Army ethics are:
1. Loyalty
2. Duty
3. Selfless-service
4. Integrity

QUESTION: What is integrity?
ANSWER: Integrity is being honest and upright, avoiding deception, and living the values you suggest for soldiers.

QUESTION: What are some ethical dilemmas?
ANSWER: Some ethical dilemmas are:
- Not caring how a task is done, as long as it gets done
- Saying there is no excuse for failure
- Maintaining a blindly can-do mindset regardless of reality
- Insisting on zero defects
- Covering up errors to look good to superiors
- Telling superiors what they want to hear, rather than the truth

- Making reports say what your leader wants to read, rather than the truth
- Setting goals that are impossible to reach
- Being loyal to those of higher rank, and not to subordinates

QUESTION: What are the four steps of an ethical decision-making process for thinking through ethical dilemmas?

ANSWER: The four steps of an ethical decision-making process for thinking through ethical dilemmas are:

1. Interpret the situation.
2. Analyze all the factors and forces that relate to the dilemma.
3. Choose the course of ACTION you believe will best serve the nation.
4. Implement the course of ACTION you have chosen.

QUESTION: What are the six forces that influence decision-making?

ANSWER: The six forces that influence decision-making are:
1. Laws, orders, and regulations
2. Basic national values
3. Traditional Army values
4. Unit operating values
5. Your values
6. Institutional pressure

QUESTION: What is the noncommissioned officer education system (NCOES) designed to do?

ANSWER: The NCOES is designed to prepare NCOs for specific levels of unit leadership.

QUESTION: What is the most essential element of combat power?

ANSWER: The most essential element of combat power is leadership.

QUESTION: How can successful leaders prepare for war?

ANSWER: Successful leaders can prepare for war by training and leading the same way they would intend to fight in a war.

QUESTION: Name the general who said, "Leadership is intangible, therefore no other weapon ever designed can replace it."

ANSWER: General Omar N. Bradley made this statement.

QUESTION: What will help the leader accomplish missions and care for his/her soldiers?

ANSWER: The factors and principles of leadership will help the leader accomplish missions and care for his/her soldiers.

QUESTION: What is duty concerning ethics?

ANSWER: Duty concerning ethics is a legal or moral obligation to do what should be done without being told to do it.

QUESTION: What is loyalty?

ANSWER: Loyalty is supporting the military and civilian chain of command, sharing commitment among soldiers for one another and placing the unit's needs and goals ahead of your own.

QUESTION: What is selfless-service?

ANSWER: Selfless-service is putting the nation's welfare and mission accomplishment ahead of the personal safety of you and your troops.

QUESTION: What are the goals of the officers and NCOs?

ANSWER: The goals of the officers and NCOs are to accomplish their unit's mission.

QUESTION: What determines the particular duties of officers and NCOs?

ANSWER: Traditions, functions, and laws determine the particular duties of officers and NCOs.

QUESTION: Whom are the commissioned officers appointed by?

ANSWER: The commissioned officers are appointed by the President of the United States.

QUESTION: Whom are the warrant officers appointed by?

ANSWER: The warrant officers are appointed by the Secretary of the Army.

QUESTION: Who delegates the authority NCOs need to get the mission accomplished?

ANSWER: The officers delegate the authority NCOs need to get the mission accomplished.

QUESTION: What must officers give to the NCOs so they can carry out their duties?

ANSWER: Officers must give NCOs the guidance, resources, assistance, and supervision necessary for them to perform their duties.

QUESTION: What is the responsibility of NCOs toward officers?

ANSWER: When helping officers carry out their duties, NCOs are responsible for assisting and advising the officers.

QUESTION: What does the mission demand that officers and NCOs do together?

ANSWER: The mission demands that officers and NCOs work together and advise, assist, and learn from one another.

QUESTION: What must officers and NCOs do at all levels?

ANSWER: Officers and NCOs must continually communicate with one another at all levels.

Keep in Touch . . .
On the Web!

www.impactpublications.com
www.ishoparoundtheworld.com
www.travel-smarter.com
www.contentfortravel.com
www.winningthejob.com
www.veteransworld.com
www.contentforcareers.com